COPPERNICKEL

number 30 / spring 2020

EDITOR/MANAGING EDITOR
Wayne Miller

CO-EDITOR
Joanna Luloff

POETRY EDITORS
Brian Barker
Nicky Beer

FICTION EDITOR
Teague Bohlen

CONSULTING EDITORS: FICTION
Alexander Lumans
Christopher Merkner

CONSULTING EDITOR: NONFICTION
Nicole Piasecki

DIGITAL CONTENT EDITOR
Kyra Scrimgeour

SENIOR EDITORS
Ashley Bockholdt
Kat Carlton
Karl Chwe
Darryl Ellison
Greg Ferbrache
Jack Gialanella
Kayla Gropp
LeShaye Hernandez
Christina Homer
Holly McCloskey
Lyn Poats
Amanda Pruess

ASSOCIATE EDITORS
Ahja Fox
Kira Morris
Angela Sapir
Karley Sun
Diego Ulibarri
Alec Witthohn

ASSISTANT EDITORS
Alex Gillow
Lauren Lopez-Ota
Brenda Pfeifer
Ember-Reece Richardson
Nicole Wood

INTERNS
Nakwisi Alderete
Ven Hickenbottom

CONTRIBUTING EDITORS
Robert Archambeau
Mark Brazaitis
Geoffrey Brock
A. Papatya Bucak
Victoria Chang
Martha Collins
Robin Ekiss
Tarfia Faizullah
V. V. Ganeshananthan
Kevin Haworth
Joy Katz
David Keplinger
Jesse Lee Kercheval
Jason Koo
Thomas Legendre
Randall Mann
Adrian Matejka
Pedro Ponce
Kevin Prufer
Frederick Reiken
James Richardson
Emily Ruskovich
Eliot Khalil Wilson

ART CONSULTANTS
Kealey Boyd
Maria Elena Buszek

OFFICE MANAGERS
Jenny Dunnington
Francine Olivas-Zarate

Copper Nickel is the national literary journal housed at the University of Colorado Denver. Published in March and October, it features poetry, fiction, essays, and translation folios by established and emerging writers. Fiction is edited by Teague Bohlen and Joanna Luloff; nonfiction is edited by Joanna Luloff and Wayne Miller; poetry is edited by Brian Barker, Nicky Beer, and Wayne Miller. We welcome submissions from all writers and currently pay $30 per printed page. Submissions are assumed to be original and unpublished. To submit, visit coppernickel.submittable.com. Subscriptions are also available—and at discounted rates for students—at coppernickel.submittable.com. *Copper Nickel* is distributed nationally through Publishers Group West (PGW) and Media Solutions, LLC, and digitally catalogued by EBSCO. We are deeply grateful for the support of the Department of English and the College of Liberal Arts & Sciences at the University of Colorado Denver. For more information, visit **copper-nickel.org**.

CONTENTS

APHORISMS

FICTION

NONFICTION

POETRY

TRANSLATION FOLIOS

Tomasz Różycki

On the Cover / Kate Petley, *Somewhere Out There*
Archival Print and Acrylic on Canvas, 48 x 52 inches, 2018

(for more on Petley's work, visit:
http://katepetley.com)

KIRSTEN KASCHOCK

Pronouncement

The world is dying I say. As a poet
            I say the world is dying and I say I
      have a job—dying being both irrevocable

and beautiful because of its irrevocability.

I get specific with the dying world. I learn
            only those things nouns objects
      of the world capable of the process *to die*

are dying. In other words—

not rocks. Species I say, being
            a poet, species who are what cannot fuck
      or (more definitively) who cannot

produce offspring outside themselves—

species are cutting out like this is a bad
            party, as if they were coupons to some
      other Safeway. Species have had it

some of them. The world's dying is for realz.

I say this and still am not satisfied.
            The satisfaction I expected to feel
      when I said something true

and final as a poet, that satisfaction

did not come. I am left unsatisfied.
            Struck dumb. This must be why
      the children. Poets should not have them

I've been told, not inasmuch as children are off-

spring produced by fucking around inside
              the self. Those should be the poems.
        I suppose if I had children (and I think

I did) I had them because though I knew

the world was dying, I thought
              I was incapable as a poet of
        being, I mean, truly being

in the world—and thus we'd be immune.

JENNIFER HABEL

A Small Movement of Freedom Inside of Fate

Ask the fox about her workday and she'll tell you about a massacre in 13th century
France.

Ask the fox about the sufficiency of love and she'll tell you she's always thinking of
the big bang.

Like all foxes, the fox is wary.

She sits at the edge of her floral sofa.

She does not unclasp her hands.

The fox can see the expressions beneath our expressions.

She hears the silence beneath our noise.

In her deep and husky voice, the fox says *primitive*: "We're such primitive creatures."
She says *nature*: Her mother "did what her nature prescribed."

Ask the fox about her novels and she'll tell you she finds geology so aesthetically
and metaphorically pleasing—these great events in the earth in turmoil.

The fox knows turmoil.

Her third husband says her father was worse than her mother.

Though old, the fox is agile.

You've got to pick up your bed and walk, she says.

She knows life is impersonal.

No, the fox has never had any female role models.

No, she cannot feel herself part of any group.

Once upon a time the fox worked for a magician.

Once upon a time she drove a crane.

Once upon a time she made "quick intense love in dark courtyards" with a Corsican
politician.

Once upon a time she felt she had to say yes to men, and women too.

Truth, that's what I care about, says the fox, who learned the necessity of judgment.

The fox's home has many exits.

She knows she's just passing through.

STEVEN KLEINMAN

Domesticant

The dog circled the block looking for a place
to shit. The dog, on a leash, looked back
over her shoulder at her master. She said *master*
with her eyes, eyes hanging out of her head,
throat pulled tight by the leash, said *master there is grass*
almost everywhere, but I cannot choose where to squat.
The master loved the dog more than anything.
Said you could shit in the house and I'd only scold.
Said you could run away and I'd only dream.
The two of them walked past an old woman.
They walked past a boy wearing a white shirt.
It was the weekend. Past the street the houses
danced, dipped then swayed. Past the street
the music raised its head then went silent.
The roofs were falling. Wires crawled like snakes
out of trashcans. The cement climbed out of itself.
Mice and rats fell dead from the phone lines,
lay decomposing, stinking sweet and surrounded by flies.
You see, the master said to the dog, *shifts in the base*
are never without costs. The master dropped
the leash at a corner and the dog stopped
without the counter pull she felt comfort in,
then she turned back toward him to wait.

HELENA BELL

Radium Girls

I.

W<small>E WERE HIRED BY</small> U.S. Radium Corporation just out of high school, my sister Alice and me, to be dial painters. They had us draw our names on a sheet of paper just to make sure we were literate, then told us were going to paint tiny, radioluminescent numerals on watch faces. Watches that were later sent to soldiers on the front.

The factory paid us 1 ½ cents per piece. It was close to home and our father liked that we would be working in a studio, like we were sculptors or watercolorists. Our mother liked that we worked inside. That we wore long skirts and shirtwaists and smocks. At the end of the day, our hands were dusty but uncalloused. It was skilled, delicate work. We were valuable. We were healthy, no girl over 25.

Everyone knew the benefits of radium. Radium was good for the skin. It killed germs. It cured impotence, arthritis, gout, and toothaches. Department stores in the city sold Tho-Radia cosmetics, straight from Paris: powders, creams, lipsticks, and toothpaste. Radium rejuvenated the cells, opened pores, cured boils, pimples, and redness. Our factory sold the residue of radium ore to be used as sand for children's play boxes. It was the most hygienic of materials.

There was radium butter and radium chocolate from Germany, though you couldn't find that in stores after the war started. Perhaps some people could: the ones who went to radium spas, took radium pills.

The paint we used was Undark and you could buy kits for do-it-yourself glow-in-the-night-like-a-ghost projects. We painted dials on watch faces, then on instrument panels for ships, planes, and other machines. All part of the war effort. The numbers on the watches would glow faint, faint green so the boys living in trenches would know when to charge, when to sleep, and when to stand-to for the morning hate.

Later, we worked on the clockworks.

There were all sorts at the factory: pretty blonde girls, plain girls, girls with thick accents and thick waists. Our fathers were bakers and masons; our mothers worked in housekeeping. We all wanted to marry soldiers.

Sometimes, on a whim, a girl would scratch her name and address on one of the watchfaces and a few months later she'd receive a letter from a boy on the front. The girl would write back, and the boy too, and after a while all of us had pen pals or relationships, depending on how serious we were.

My friend Katherine had seven boys she wrote to. They all had single syllable names like Tom or Bill or Jack. Four were regular infantry, standing knee deep in mud and pointing their rifles across the mist and waiting. Two were clockworks. One didn't say. Katherine wrote to them all about Orange and the factory and the other girls and all our families. We did little to distinguish the lines between us. The time one of us was chased through a department store by a bee appeared in all our letters. "My sister Alice was telling me the other day," Katherine wrote. We knew the boys were unlikely to compare notes on us, and if they did, we didn't care.

Some girls made promises: they talked about children and spring and the flowers they dreamed of for a wedding. I asked lots of questions: what were their homes like, their childhoods. Katherine avoided anything personal. She talked about the weather and vaudeville shows. She told them there were other boys she wrote to, but she never mentioned their names. If her letters ran short, she finished the page with drawings: cats and birds and dogs.

The boys who wrote to Katherine drew animals of their own: rats and fat frogs and carrier pigeons. They said there were other girls they wrote to too. Girls from home; girls they'd known since they were young. Girls they'd sat behind in church while imagining the weight of their hair, the tension of those curls. Like the boys, all these girls had one syllable names: Jane or June or Joan. And the boys had pet names for them like June-bug or Joannie.

It meant something different, we thought, when a boy lengthened a girl's name, one that was meant to be tight and terse on the lips, to add cadence and rhythm to a name that didn't ask for it. It wasn't the same for boys—who must have had long names already: Thomas, William, Jackson—for whom it was nothing to cut it short.

It mattered somehow, this choice. It mattered because your preference for a person could depend entirely on the shape, the sound of you in someone else's mouth.

All the boys promised to visit us when they came home, but we never expected it. We were used to the idea of ships leaving full of brown uniforms, trucks, ammunitions, and food. The Atlantic was one long conveyor of American goods and services. Even Katherine, with her seven boys neatly stacked up in piles on her writing desk, never considered she would have to face one.

The first clockwork arrived on a Tuesday. We'd never seen one in person, just the bits and pieces that came through the factory. There weren't pictures of them in the papers or posters. People who knew people who'd seen them said they looked like divers: the metal casing and bell helmet. They couldn't talk inside the suit, not like a normal person. They communicated through clicks and whistles, whirs and pops. We supposed they could try to talk like normal, they still had mouths and faces and somewhere underneath, but it came out muffled as if from very far, or very deep, like the rustling of paper in a schoolroom you still dreamed of.

So when the clockwork came in, we didn't know how to understand him. He had one of Katherine's letters in his hand, so we knew she was the one he was looking for. She asked him to wait outside till she was ready to leave, and he did.

When a girl first started working at the studio, she liked to paint her eyes and lips. Neighborhood boys loved to see us lit up like ghosts in the dark. We thought perhaps the clockwork would be the same, and so we surrounded Katherine and combed her hair with our paint powdered fingers. We painted her eyes, rubbed her cheeks, her arms, and patted the curves of her dress until she was luminous: gold and glowing as the soldier who waited for her.

And while we primped and petted her, another clockwork walked in. Then another. One with a letter from Katherine, one with a letter from me. Katherine and I decided Alice should join us, and the girls painted our lips, our hair, our dresses, and hands.

The clockworks didn't seem to care which of us was which. We walked together in a big group, with Katherine and Alice and me somewhere between the three of them.

Sometimes they didn't seem to understand us when we spoke to them. We asked questions and pointed out landmarks, and they stared at us and didn't say a thing.

When they clustered together, then separated, we had a hard time telling them apart, though perhaps it didn't matter as I barely knew my clockwork. His first letter had been only two months before and we'd barely progressed past the "Hello, my name is Edward" stage. He wanted to study physics after the war. He missed his parents. He hated rats. He was meaning to apologize to his sister but hadn't worked up to it yet. Maybe talking to another girl would give him the practice he needed.

People stared at us. The clockworks were three times our size and they stomped their feet so hard your teeth rattled and dogs barked. People crossed the street to avoid us. When you stood close to them, if you pressed your ear against their chests, you could hear the ticking from all the gears inside. By the end of the evening, when we were braver, we ran our hands against their backs, checking for seams. We couldn't find any. And the more we paid attention, the more we noticed the quiet: their joints didn't creak. Their legs and arms didn't whine or rasp. Only when foot after foot came down, hard, against the cobblestones did they make any noise. They were like children splashing in puddles, enjoying the novelty of walking in the open, of grass and pavement and soil.

After sunset, the clockworks took us to the waterfront. They lifted us by our waists and perched us like birds on their shoulders, to give us a better view of the ships sailing in and out of the port. Or perhaps so the ships could better see us: the glowing girls on burnished steeds. The next morning, I checked my skin in the mirror, expecting to see big purple marks where their hands had gripped us. There was none, they'd been so gentle it was as if we'd never met them at all.

II.

IN THE BEGINNING, clockworks were called Goldens. After the Somme, after the Land-ships Committee with their tanks, the caterpillar tracks rolling over wire and mud and frogs and rats, after the explosion at Messines with its 10,000 in ten minutes, the British on the hilltops watching ankle bones and jaws fly up into the air and back down, the British in London startling in the streets, and after it should have ended, but didn't, they made the Goldens.

Imagine, they said, a soldier who could be wound up and set on his course: at Ypres and Verdun, through bullets and whizzbangs and he didn't stop to eat, or sleep, impervious to gas, and imagine if we had a section of such men, a battalion, a Golden Brigade, a golden tide of metal and rifles and hand grenades sweeping across the line and straight on till morning. Imagine it, they said, what we could do with such things.

The first Goldens were former tank commanders: men who'd lived in small spac-es filled with ammunition and oil, signaling equipment and a crate of pigeons, sol-diers' kits and food: bread loaves, cheese, tea, sugar, and milk. Men who could bear the din and the roar and the tang of metal on their tongues.

More soldiers came. Some clockworks, and some infantry who could smoke with us and tell jokes. We asked them about the clockworks, but they knew less than we did. Clockworks were on a different schedule: patrolling and digging tunnels and laying wire. They were never seen with guns, but they must have been issued.

"Probably don't think they need them," a boy from Virginia said. "They're metal through and through."

When I was young, my mother owned a tabby cat named Tiger. Tiger like to sleep near a particular tree where mockingbirds liked to nest. When Tiger showed up, the mockingbirds would dive at him, raking their talons against his back, over and over again while Tiger stretched and flicked his tail and let them come at him until they exhausted themselves.

Once, walking home from the studio I saw a clockwork standing on a street cor-ner as if waiting for the carriages and cars to pass to give him space to cross. But even when the traffic slowed, he didn't move. He waited until some neighborhood boys came up to him and asked if he needed help. Was he lost? Was he waiting for some-one? Looking? Did he have orders to stand there and protect this particular street corner, this particular condemned apartment building, this particular grocery stand from the Germans? From the Russians? From Austria? Hungary? The Martians?

Could he even hear them? Did he see them standing there, asking their questions?

When the clockwork didn't answer, they started yelling at him, pushing. Did he feel anything? Did he know anything? They beat their hands against his back and the clockwork swayed back and forth.

I left before the boys did, but they saw me later, coming home with gold light in my hair. I knew the clockworks, didn't I? Were they all broken? I shrugged and kept walking.

"Are you broken too?"

III.

MEN AND WOMEN came to the factory with pamphlets and lectures and questions about the frequency of our menstrual cycles. They told us we all had anemia and recommended bed rest. A girl in the factory broke her jaw after tripping on some stairs. Her face withered in on itself, then she died.

"It was phosphorous," the men and women said. "Doctors have confirmed it was phosphorous. From another plant where she used to work."

On his next visit, I brought Edward home with me. He sat on one whole side of the kitchen table and we passed him the potatoes and corn. He couldn't eat any of it, at least we never saw him try, but he took small portions to put on his plate. Either out of politeness, or the familiarity of the movement, we supposed. By then they'd improved the design so that words could sometimes appear in flickering glowing paint across his face. I still couldn't have a real conversation with him, but it was nice to know that there was something human, something thinking, somewhere inside. Alice flinched anytime a word appeared, the lines and curlicues dancing in some indecipherable message until it stilled, then changed again. One night I thought I saw the words *rose quartz, Bangalore,* and *the warm winter,* but they changed too quickly for me to be sure.

"Will the war be over soon?" Alice asked.

Edward lifted his shoulders, then dropped them.

"I read somewhere that you can talk to each other across great distances. Like radio signals. Is that true?"

He lifted his shoulders, dropped them.

"Can you understand me?"

The same gesture.

"Are you talking to someone right now?" she asked. "How long is your range? A mile? Two? Three thousand? Do you think they can hear you? The boys on the other side of the sea?"

He passed the plates along and didn't answer her at all.

Afterwards he took me to the wharf and held my hand. There could be subs out there, I thought, and yet we stood watching the waves, both of us bright as Christmas.

"Is this what it's like on the front? Standing before the black, lighting the way home?"

He said nothing, did nothing, when I shivered in the cold.

IV.

THE GOLDENS WERE sent with other sections to the firing line. Eight days on the front, then eight days in support, then eight days billeted in a farmhouse or town. Like clockwork they stood at attention for the stand-to, the morning hate. They were told when to stand up, to sit down. First they were too tall, then not tall enough. They were sentries, then miners. They were shields. Sometimes the other soldiers whispered among themselves that if they had snipers, and Fritz had snipers, and if they had miners, and Fritz had snipers, and rats and lice and mortars and biscuits and ration trains, then Fritz must have Goldens too. And how could we tell them apart?

"Every few months you show up even though we say we don't want you or need you. Every few months. Like clockwork."

At Artois, a section of Goldens were sent out at dawn as part of a raid. The first one fell just a few yards out of the trench, his hands and feet sunk so far in the mud it took ten men to drag him back in again. The next two didn't fare much better: ten yards across, maybe twenty. The Captain wouldn't send anyone out in daylight and the whole line watched as German snipers pinged bullets off the Goldens' heads and haunches until nightfall.

V.

DURING THE LONG hours in the studio, the girls compared stories with each other. What the metal tasted like if you kissed it. How you could only tell whether they were happy or not by an acrid smell they sometimes gave off. Like metal grinding against metal. Like chemicals burning. We knew if we opened them up, pushed deep enough, we would find flesh and bone. Arteries and nerves. All of their pieces had to be left inside, otherwise the process could never be reversed. It could be reversed, couldn't it?

"Have you ever been touching one when he's startled by something?" Hazel asked. "You get a tingling at the tip of your tongue. You can't scrape it off, even later. I wonder if they feel that all the time. If it's why they're so quiet."

When the war ended and the clockworks came home, they went on a list. It was easier to put a man in a golden case than to take him back out again. Older soldiers and wounded went first. The rest had to wait.

Edward was young and healthy and the Veterans Bureau said it could be until spring so he stayed in a rented room in the city.

Alice began meeting with the Consumer League and led a protest, which closed a factory outside of Orange. Benzene poisoning. Then she started working as a research assistant on industrial diseases and at dinner would tell us all about hatter's shakes and brass founder's ague. Miner's asthma, painter's colic, loony gas. She told us about septicemia and necrosis, of phossy jaw and carotted gums. The bone could become so porous it would collapse like sand. She'd seen a dentist pull an entire mandible out of someone's mouth, like unloosing a hinge. I told her phosphorous wasn't in the paint we used.

I didn't want to upset Alice, so Edward and I dined out. Only he wouldn't eat, and I wasn't hungry so instead we went to parks and fed ducks and geese small bits of bread. We passed a sheet of paper back and forth, writing out our responses to each other.

VI.

THERE WERE A few things the soldiers thought the Goldens were good for. At night, huddled in the trenches, their bodies glowed. It wasn't bright enough to see by, but standing really close to one, you could hold out your arm and check for lice. You could also hear the tick tick tick of their wiring and gears. To some it was almost like being at home, sitting on the floor of the living room and staring at the clock their grandparents had brought over on a boat from Europe.

Edward wrote that the soldiers never figured out that the ticking was intentional. It was a sound they made themselves, a cluck cluck cluck with their mouths.

Edward never knew the names of the other Goldens. He didn't know where they were from, if they had girls back home or sisters or brothers. But he always assumed they had parents. He thought about writing it out to ask them, but there was a comfort in the quiet. When he woke in the hospital, my name was the first he saw, scratched on his wrist like graffiti. It annoyed him at first. Less than a day in a new body and someone had already claimed it.

His first assignment was Ploegsteert. There were raids in the morning, shelling during the day. His NCO used to offer him rum, even though Edward couldn't drink it.

"It was quiet before you got here," he said. "Live and let live. But you and your friends . . . it's different now."

At the end of the war, most people heard the story of the Christmas truce. It was a nice story to tell: Germans and English playing football in No Man's Land.

But there was also the breakfast truce. The ration train truce. The truce of "no one shoot the latrines." For three months the English ran out of shells, and the Germans responded by not sending any over of their own. When the Saxons held the line, it was quiet. When the Prussians were set to relieve them, the Saxons told the Anglos to "give 'em hell."

The ones who survived the war were the ones most able to shoot at the people who were shooting at them: the ones who got past the uncanny valley, the enemy who looked like him but was different. The enemy who ate breakfast, slept in the cold, got bitten by rats and lice and hated High Command and asked for newspapers when they didn't trust their own and sent over messages in fake mortars, who sometimes sent warnings and sometimes still came over the top with a gun and bayonet as much as he said he didn't want to.

Even trained, as they were, soldiers only hit one target out of four. Command's first priority was making sure that the men acted at war.

This was a story Edward overheard:

An Australian section, first day on the front, watched a German soldier walk away from the trench and back towards support. Probably on leave, the Australians thought. Headed to his sweetheart in Berlin. Two weeks vacation. They watched his pack bounce as he walked. He wasn't even wearing a helmet.

One of the Australians said it'd serve him right if he got shot. One of the others said he was too far away.

"I could do it," he said.

"No you couldn't."

It went back and forth until the one grabbed his rifle and set it against the parapet. He sighted. He fired. The German didn't even twitch. Just kept on walking.

"Told you," the other said.

The first Australian, red-faced, scrambled out of the trench and onto his belly, right in front. In full view of the Germans.

"Now you're gonna get yourself killed."

"No I won't," he said.

He sighted again. He fired. The German fell.

The first Australian got back in the trench and went to cleaning his gun. He kept his head down as his fingers worked automatically, quick and punctuated. They never faltered. The others stood over him and assured him that they saw other Germans climbing out now. They were pulling their friend below. He was helping himself. He was fine. He'd have to write his sweetheart, say he'd be a little late. But he'd be fine. He was fine. He was fine.

Edward replayed the story over and over in his head. How the German soldier stood up, brushed himself off, and wrapped a bandage around his calf and went on with his day. He was somewhere in Germany now, with his girl. She'd check the bandage and rewind it for him. When he had children, he would show them the scar. He'd tell them how it almost kept him from their mother.

And as Edward replayed the story in his head, he learned to breathe slowly in and out. He learned to whistle against the inside of his helmet and disturb the paint that made him and the other soldiers glow. It was like blowing grains of sand across a glass table, he thought. And it would settle into its own shapes. Sometimes he even imagined it could form words.

When Edward was 16, he purchased a wooden recurve bow with his own money he'd earned working for a neighbor. He told his sister he was going to shoot a deer with it. A buck. Big enough to eat all winter. His sister had laughed at him and said he wouldn't be able to kill a squirrel with a puny thing like that.

The first three days, Edward didn't see a deer, a squirrel, and barely even a bird. He thought he heard a bear once, and he'd scrambled up the nearest tree as quick as he could before he remembered that bears could climb too.

On the fourth, Edward finally spotted a deer through the trees and took his shot. The deer turned as the string whipped by his ear and the arrow plunged into the deer's femoral artery rather than its heart. Edward tracked it for a hundred yards, listening to it scream. When it finally collapsed, Edward tried to break its neck, leaning on its shoulder and twisting the head as quick as he could. It didn't work and finally he sat down with his back against a tree, the animal leaning against him as the blood ran out. His sister screamed at him saying he should've known to bring a gun. It wasn't kind to the animal, knowing it was going to die, and Edward just sitting there. Waiting.

VII.

Alice got Katherine to join her in a lawsuit, and some of the other girls too. The factory let me go after I gave them a list of names of other girls who'd left over the years: girls with broken bones and migraines. I told her about Katherine's cousin who wore dentures but had to spit them out most days. Our supervisor had said she must have gotten syphilis from one of the Army men and then he fired her. For public health reasons, he'd said.

When Edward asked how I was getting along, I lied. His surgery had been scheduled and I didn't want him to worry. I told him that the best brushes were sable, a species of marten found in mountain forests: Russia or China, the Ursuls. I told him how each hair must remember the shaking off of winter snow, must long for it, and I mimed bringing the tip to my mouth, stroking it against my tongue.

I told him the paint tasted a little like pennies because I thought that was a taste he would know. I didn't tell him how I'd started to crave it at the end, sucking hard candies between shifts even though they cracked my teeth and made my gums bleed.

He found out anyway, through the paper. They ran a picture of Katherine with her sparse hair pinned back beneath a cloche hat. There was nothing about the work we'd done, about the clockworks or the war, only our miscarriages and our deaths.

Edward came straight to the courthouse from the doctor. He was thin and pale against the back wall, shrugging his shoulders up and down so that I could recognize him.

We went out to dinner and he ordered a manhattan. He said he'd never had alcohol before, but he could hear other men in the trenches talk about the drinks they remembered having, the drinks they'd have again. He laughed a little and said he wasn't sure if they were telling the truth, or if they were just repeating things they'd heard themselves. Maybe no one on the whole front had ever done anything except grow up, leave their parents, and muck through France, then Belgium.

His voice was reedy, like whistling. I'd imagined something deeper, richer, darker, a voice to hide in. I'd imagined him with an accent. I thought he'd say words like "ma'am" and "Bubba."

I thought he might ask me to marry him, and practiced saying no over and over again. But he never did. I told myself he had options, and the whole world to love him now that he'd been cracked open and pulled out, now that a doctor had stripped away wires and springs, brushed matted hair and bits of paper from his forehead: all that made him special curling on the floor like ash. Somewhere among the filings would have been my name, swept up and thrown away.

Katherine and Alice settled the lawsuit, and there's a standard now for provable suffering, but they can't take it out of us. At the trial, a woman took the stand and explained how the body treated radium like calcium. It was absorbed by the bones and degraded the marrow. I pictured my bones like a bird's: hollow and crisscrossed by struts and trusses, like a series of trenches allowing movement forward and back. Half-life by half-life.

The night before he went home, Edward told me he would run into German soldiers on patrol. Fritz wasn't allowed to fire. It would reveal position and then a whizzbang or machine gun would find them. It'd kill them both. The Goldens never carried weapons so they couldn't fire if they wanted to. If there was just one German, he'd turn and run. If there were two, sometimes they'd jump Edward and try to force his head into the mud. Force him to breathe it in until he choked. Edward would stand there as they beat him with their hands and fists. Then, when they had tired themselves out, Edward would push their faces into the ground, same as they'd tried to do to him. He pressed them so deep that sometimes only their hands would stick up at the end, their white fingers dirt smudged and broken, twisted up like roots entangled in the soil.

I thought of reassuring him: he couldn't do that now. Not with his strength gone, the certainty of his place. I wanted to reassure us both: to picture him one day standing by an open window, peering through the darkness in hope that he might see a ghost beckoning him from the distance.

Instead I told him that one day he'll have a daughter. He should name her after his sister; then she'll forgive him.

And when she's born, press your ear to her chest, Edward. How strong her heartbeat, how precise, each one connected, driven, luminous with promise.

Is it time?

Is it time?

Is it time?

EDWARD HIRSCH

The Black Dress

I don't know why I opened her book
almost randomly, on a whim,
it signaled me from the shelf
after all these years, like a burning
black dress tangled in the branches,
her dress, she was the one
who was burning,
and that's when the letter fell out,
a love letter, sort of, after we'd given up
on each other, or did we?,
our impossibility,
and suddenly it came back to me
in a rush, that night in Boston,
a restaurant on the harbor, a storm
simmering outside, that slinky
black dress she was wearing,
I didn't know she was burning
inside of it, I thought
it was the coming storm,
summer lightning,
I didn't know I was turning
the pages of her book, her body,
which I would read so closely,
I wanted it so desperately,
she was the fire, I didn't know
she was already mourning
for her childhood in the orchard,
her lost self, forgive me,
I didn't know she was burning
when she took off that black dress.

SHAKTHI SHRIMA

Real Girl

John Everett Millais, "Ophelia," 1852. Oil on Canvas.
Tate Modern (permanent collection), London

They say she's singing, but her body
      is too slack for sound—strange, pale shock
suddening the river and yet the river's welcomed

      her with all its murk and stutter, for her it's narrowed itself
into a second skirt. Did she even mean to drown?

      No—she just wanted to be held. Seeing the water's dark

steady muscle she could only shiver into it, her hymns coming undone
      in the bank's sharp chorus of reeds. But then the river steals her waist—
to memorize her, or hunt for whatever's left of her song—slowly

      it swallows, no witness to its meal but the moon, then the sun,
then the moon. Choked halfway into the earth she's stunned silent,

      finally a real girl. Everything that sees her hungers
like the river hungers. Flowers unhip themselves

      toward her upturned palms, unable to bear
their own color. The shrubs throng together,
      brawling shadows to covet what the water still

hasn't consoled. You're among the daily tourists that squint
      into the blond wood of her frame—*Ophelia*,
patron saint of gift-shop memorabilia,

her name the name of every grief you try to vanish by calling gorgeous.
      In the painting she's alone and gone. It doesn't matter

who she loved, or how. Say the light is moonlight.
        Say the river is anywhere you want it to be. Say the river
is the first glass of water you ever gulped down

        multiplied into the dizzy marsh of you. The river is desperate
for any color but its own. But what of her secret body—

        un-rivered and howling, joints swiveling wild? Your secret body
has a waist that cannot fit in any frame, is reckless as a prophet in a city square.
        Your secret body wants to forget that it is a body at all. The moon

mirrored in the painted water becomes a tongue wagging
        at the moon. In your mirror's frame you are tongueless. You

wane. You fountain. You second-skirt. You hunger
        with the mirror's hunger. Your secret body wears you like a burst seam
before it cannot wear you anymore. You lie in sheets printed

        with tulips. Little-spooning their wrinkled gulf,
you're covered in more flowers than a shrine

        or a grave. Who would worship something that could answer back?
The river is more than a river when she lies in it, her lips
        parted just enough that you swear that whatever sparks in the hollow

between her mouth and her sound isn't the twitch of the water's
        inevitable rising, but the echo of a lover hungrier than the water

kneeling on the bank, begging to let him dry her.

ALESSANDRA LYNCH

Best House

The best house I could make was out of Paint—
I never thought of roofs. There was relief in the dark
thick line—both enclosure and door. Something soft
crept back and forth in every house, a little nervous. Not like my "real" house
of cold miraculous angles. I made so many houses that year one bled
into the next. Blur of Houses moving fast as birds with that urge for South or slow
depending on my approach, whether or not I was an apparition.
      Ultimately, I was close to no one in the House but I was
so intimate with the House itself I absorbed the stealth of pain it absorbed—
squalor of pain, sometimes squall. Sometimes we painted ourselves
silly in pain, House and I, convergent.
      In the basement I made snails out of clay—
the ironic basement where centipedes curled. I never got
the jitters around them. They had such small faces and silent mouths.
But I worried over the House—I didn't fight in there—would it go up in flames?
And could the unsmiling faces of dolls ever
burn out?
      An impersonal blue square is my newest paint House—peek through its
trickly green door, its gold smear of window. The private openness of the square.
Its doorknob
a compass.
      Here's a jar of paint—make a real cheap house—warm and soft and roof-
less—where the sky's welcome—and starry birds—the color
of cuts in hiding—.
      That dear familiar shelter.

ALICIA MOUNTAIN

Runtime Squinting

I don't know when or how it's going to end,
this poem or this life.

The film was long, but there were some good parts.
I sat in the dark beside someone I knew,
past tense, and passed popcorn back and forth
less a fistful each time.
I wasn't hungry and became less so.
I allowed myself Dr. Pepper—
unnamable manufactured spices and sweetness.

Now my attention is held by documentary
almost exclusively.
It seems due to the higher stakes,
but I think my true lonely life
is looking for company in what's real.

We didn't know each other
in the way that you know
how someone wants to be buried
or burned or eulogized,
how many column-inches
to buy in the local paper.
Just that yours was a shoulder for my head.
Just that for a while I didn't care
that the projection bled
over the edges of the screen.
Didn't care that we had to fold in
to each other so that someone could escape
for a refill, and again when they returned.

I would like for my body to be a stand of aspen—

paper bark and on fire with yellow,
multiple and unalone.
For the part of me that leaves that body behind,
that walks out past the concession stand,
this will end in one of two ways:
surprise at how quickly
the dark night snuck up on me
while I was in some other darkness,
or surprise to find it's still so bright a day.

Sierras

I slept through the foothills and woke in a forest
of pines, tall, taller, sheer dizzying drops. Heat
found the back of my neck, even through the glass
of the car window, the height swung its lamps
in my eyes and I followed the spine of the hill
like a goat, a small white goat, feigning dominion
over rockface and scree. Such pretending
kept the swooning at bay. The too much
of an angel's long fall, wings not catching.
But there was time in the height, one
chance, another. Somewhere lavender,
intensifying in heat, farm fields in August.
I imagined a path along the mountain's ridge,
spindly as the tracks cattle will make when
someone rings the bell calling them home
on paths crooked and beautifully worn
by the ritual coming and going.
Then I looked again and the mountain
blackened as if the sun had tripped
its arc and the once beautiful angel went headlong,
wings pressed to his sides, not even trying.
Reckless. Fear of falling raced ahead of itself.
A sweat broke and I looked for a brief
minute until I refused the knowledge and looked away.

DON BOGEN

Three Rose Studies

1. An Apartment in Bordeaux

ON THE EDGE OF THE picture, the rose dissolves into words. And the words it blurs into are meaningless. They float on the canvas with no context except that they are English and thus *chic* here, and have different typefaces, dark brown against the gray background. The little fragments of etymology, meaning, and sound they spark out are just for show. The picture itself--big, obvious, luridly seductive--transcends the words because it marks a specific desire. Who wouldn't like a rose that could last for months or years, right on the wall there whenever you want to look at it?

Like the rose the picture fails to capture, you couldn't live forever. And I go on in this flattened world among photos, words, and memories like clouds I can reach my hand through--everything impalpable, vibrating a bit yet finally static.

Only music moves, and it moves me partly because I learned it from you. In the midst of it all, your voice became it. Words forming in the pitched air led toward others: phrases opening and closing in French, English, Russian, Latin carried on the chorus, you in the swirls of harmony alive with a direction to go. Music resembles the rose.

2. Terrace Avenue

THE HOUSE WE shared has roses on either side of the porch, planted, I imagine, when it was built in 1904 and nostalgic even then. One white bush, one red, each tangled and abundant in its season: hundreds of flower heads pushing out amid the curved stalks and thorns, and on each head hundreds of petals in firetruck red or pale green-ish white that spread for their days and fall off.

When you clipped some and brought them inside, the smell--waxy, way too sweet-- would always last longer than the blossoms themselves. They began to droop even before you could arrange them. The curled petals would drop in clumps on the dining room table like dozens of Post-it notes: reminders of something that was supposed to be important but had slipped into the past.

If I pick some now, I put them in the ceramic pitcher your friend made before we met. With its stenciled border reminiscent of Arts & Crafts, the pitcher has so much more resonance than the blown roses, or even the ones still on the bushes, that I want to run my hand over it before I set it back on the shelf.

3. Near the Sea

IF OBJECTS CAN be said to speak, the two mugs I bought for my parents at a tourist shop in York said more than I'd originally intended. They held stories: history, of course--the white rose on one, the red on the other—but also the junior year abroad we discovered we'd both had, though yours was before mine. When we drank from the mugs at my parents' house and I mentioned where they came from, our pasts overlapped in counterpoint.

The mugs are in a landfill somewhere. The rose shapes pressed into clay and fired will take a long time to return to the soil. My parents' bodies persisted as ash for a while at the bottom of the Pacific Ocean, and what was left of yours after medical researchers made the best use they could of it traveled down a creek to San Pablo Bay. Like music, or your voice lifting inside it, it was mostly dispersed in air.

When I move through a day entangled with words that flare and fade in their different purposes, the past shifts around me like the hot breeze off a fire. Though I want resolution and permanence, I know I am alive only in the lack of these things.

Translation Folio

MAYA TEVET DAYAN

Translator's Introduction

Jane Medved

MAYA TEVET DAYAN (BORN 1975) is an Israeli-Canadian poet and writer, who splits her time between Tel Aviv and Vancouver. She is the author of a novel *One Thousand Years To Wait* (2011) and two books of poetry: *Let There Be Evening, Let There Be Chaos* (2015), and *Wherever We Float, That's Home* (2018), the collection in which these poems first appeared.

Tevet Dayan holds a PhD in Indian Philosophy and Literature, and is herself a translator of Sanskrit Poetry. Together with her husband and their three daughters, Tevet Dayan has moved between dozens of homes in four different continents, a restlessness that infuses her poetry, as the narrator tries to find her place in the world. The speaker in these poems is a wife, but also a wanderer; a woman who freely admits that she can't stay put, either as a teenage girl or a mother of three. In poems like "Genealogy" this instability is traced to relatives who were caught by the Holocaust. But in poems such as "Australia" it is simply the speaker's need for an ever widening horizon, her addiction to the constant state of possibility.

Generations of women inhabit Tevet Dayan's work, where relationships are not bounded by the physical universe. Grandmothers, great grandmothers, and her own mother, who died from cancer, advise, admonish, and applaud her throughout these poems. They form "the transparent generations / of mothers and daughters who rose / and slept their lives between light and darkness / from sleep to awakening to sleep" ("My Daughter Is the Gateway to the Night"). They hand down wisdom, argue with each other, and suggest that the speaker might want to wash the floor. The kitchen table, a pot of soup, the dog's wet nose– this is the stuff of the poet's magical world, as she ponders reincarnation and the growing piles of laundry with equal passion.

These poems span the range from Tevet Dayan's early childhood years into the present day. Perhaps the strongest narrative thread in this collection is the illness and early death of Tevet Dayan's mother, a loss she is still writing about. Sometimes the speaker is herself a mother, sometimes a motherless child. Sometimes she is both at once, confronting the terrible responsibility of love. Times and places may change, but the focus remains the same—family, with its constraint and opportunities, protects and restricts. Family defines you. And family allows you to grow.

What attracted me most in Tevet Dayan's work is her creation of parallel and sometimes conflicting realities: childhood innocence masks loss and trauma, the present is inhabited by messengers from the past, the familiar becomes strange, and the strange is revealed to be expected and commonplace. Nothing can be taken for granted, since reality is not a solid platform, but a living entity, layered and shifting. This is a world of the seen and the unseen. Here, the physical and the spiritual are on equal footing.

I love the sense of faith in these poems, of another larger presence working behind the scenes. Tevet Dayan's work is rich with myth, fable, apocryphal stories, family legend and biblical allusions. She warns us that women can be turned into trees, that karma must be accumulated, and that souls will come back to visit. She reminds us that the universe is perched precariously, there are unequal measures of light and dark, but long ago, God promised "It will be good."

Hiding

I want to write about that door,
the front door I opened with the hands
of an eight year old, a fifteen year old,
a twenty year old, a forty year old.
I want to tell how I hid from my mother
one Friday afternoon, when I came home
from school, still wearing my backpack.
I stood outside the door for hours
and spied on her, watching how she waited
for me to arrive: her beautiful cheeks sinking
into themselves like parachutes emptied
of air, her eyes shooting their green arrows
in every direction without hitting a thing.

She wandered between the kitchen and living room
like a pendulum, lifting then replacing
the telephone, moving her lips like a silent film star.
I didn't hear a thing through the door.
How long did I stand and watch her like that?
Until she turned grey before my eyes?
Until the evening grew dark?
Perhaps I got cold. Perhaps I had pity on her,
a door of mercy opening inside me.

My mother almost fainted in my arms,
her eyes looking towards me
as if through a hollow tunnel that had at its end
the unimaginable, the unthinkable,
that which must now be erased from her memory.
I saved her
from the gaping abyss, from the capriciousness

of life, from my disappearance
and from her own disappearance.
For the first time in my life
I felt the responsibility of being loved,
and it broke my heart.

My Mother Invites a Doctor for Lunch

He arrives at five after twelve,
during the afternoon break from the clinic,
lowering his head

in order not to hit the door frame.
The hair on the top of his head is thinning
like oxygen at the peak of a mountain.

My mother seats him in my chair,
dressed in her pastel sweater,
thrilled that he agreed to come.
She believes in co-existence

with physicians.
The yellow winter light enters
through the geranium pot on the window,
and pours onto our backpacks
strewn around the kitchen floor,
the doctor glances down

to the painted tiles
that my parents bought in Jaffa.
My mother says "Make yourself at home,"
and immediately there is the span

of a desert between us.
She serves chicken soup, asks if he
would also like carrots,
when is he planning to get married,
how did he decide to become a doctor,
how long does it take to get here
from the village every morning.

He sips the soup
without a sound. It would be possible
to imagine he's not even there,

if he wasn't as tall as the minaret of a mosque
in the middle of our dining room.

What did we know about Arabs?
That they murder women and children,
they shout, they water down gasoline,
sell horse meat, have arranged marriages,
that they have no idea what love is.

The Doctor says thank you and agrees
to another serving. My sister and I
watch his hand and how the spoon arrives
at his mouth precisely, lifting from the bowl
like an airplane taking off above
an ocean of boiling soup, being swallowed

in a different universe.
Under his heavy eyelashes stretches
the line of a far horizon, his gaze
looking through us. We are scared
to ask ourselves, what does he know about Jews?

Afterwards, he bends over again,
drooping like a flower stem, on his way out.
My mother invites him to come back soon.
"Of course," he says.
But he never does. He turns instead

to his own future—
the village, the wedding, the continuation
of his balding, the traffic jams, and his promotion
to director of the clinic,
and my mother turns to her future—

to live, become sick and die young
and in between—
pots empty and fill
like hearts,
and bowls follow the necessary path
of cupboard-table-sink-cupboard,

orbiting the kitchen
that has become our world.

I only saw him once more,
years later, when I stood at the entrance
to his office, trying to get a prescription
for my mother, that he wouldn't agree to give me.
He explained about the new regulations
as if he didn't know
what love was. I screamed at him.
What I wouldn't give for a happy ending.

I remember that moment clearly:
me and my crying and everything I knew about doctors
and mothers, slipping out of me,
bubbling, boiled sadness.

Three Years Since Your Death

The leaves of the maple tree in my garden
are red and damp from the rain.
I have stopped expecting to see the sun-
bathed nuts you loved, between its branches.
I drive a car much larger than I need. The street
signs are written in the mother tongue of others.
Yellow traffic lights sway beneath their wires,
but there is no wind and no promise of wind.
I turn a key inside the lock of a house
built by strangers, for people who are not you,
and not me, in a time that preceded both of us.
I know how to point out four kinds of wheat
in English, and to choose bread from a bakery
where there is not one thing from the ground
where you are buried, from where you bore me.
I have learned the movements of a frozen winter,
vaster and stiller than the winter that held you
in its arms as you passed from your body.
Where did you go? Where did I go?

If we ran into each other in the street today,
you would ask *Is that you?* And perhaps
I wouldn't know how to answer.

—*translated from the Hebrew by Jane Medved*

LUCAS SOUTHWORTH

The Crying Rooms

THE VENTS EXHALED THE WHOLE way, constant and raw. The shoulder slid past. The sheared edges of what had once been fields of corn. Light from the bus's windows bent into the dark. Fall was becoming winter, the blue tinge of it cautious and slow against the glass, like a patient trying his side for the first time after surgery.

I pictured my son in the aisle seat, a book on his lap, his phone plugged into the outlet, earbuds buried in his ears. He was fourteen, still. A fascinating and beguiling age. A boy, and yet capable, capable.

I pretended to hear the music, just the seams of whatever it was he listened to.

I opened a hand to him on the armrest.

I'm your mother, I said. Tell me what you need to tell me.

But even in my imagination, my son flashed anger. He pulled his legs to his chest, his socks on the seat, his chin resting on top of his knees. He sat there until he was gone again, only a scattering of crumbs from some other passenger on the vinyl. I wanted to brush them off. I couldn't bring myself to do it. Not even with a tissue or the backs of my gloves.

Five hours of dark road became six. I kept checking my watch, though I had no real reason, no real place to be. The air circled through everyone's lungs twice, three times, four. I thought, No one can take a ride like this without a little despair. I thought, How can I continue? How do any of us continue?

The bus finally wandered into the city and stopped in a lurch and flurry of breaks. The riders all stood as if choreographed. Most filed off and into the passenger seats of idling pickups and sedans. The rest dissipated sleepily down subway steps.

I watched taillights disappear. I felt the pavement stretching, stretching.

In a diner a few blocks away, the waitress gave me a newspaper for free. It was past midnight, she said, and the man would come around again soon. He'd block the door with another bundle as he always did.

She eyed me. You're a woman alone, she said.

I'm a doctor, I told her. I know the corners of the night.

She laughed and brought my eggs while I scanned the classifieds.

They don't really put much in the paper anymore, she said.

The crying rooms, I asked, what are they?

Only heard of them, she said.

I read the ad again and picked up my fork. The eggs were perfect. Yolk filled the entire plate as soon as I cut in.

I CALLED THE number the next morning. I met the owners in the afternoon.

The man pointed me toward an armchair near the window, in the sun. He took the other, and the woman steered a rolling chair from behind a front desk that looked like it should be at a hotel or spa. On the coffee table between us sat a stack of magazines, straight and untouched. Ferns softened the lobby's edges. I noticed brass, so dull, and off-white walls, maybe even almost gray. Three paintings hung, large and framed. Sailboats upon the open sea.

From what I understood, I told them, I was perfect for the place. I'd worked nights before. I liked it. I wasn't too young or old, too talkative or quiet. I wasn't easily rattled or taken in. I had no interest in family or being liked or making friends.

The owners didn't bring up that I was overqualified. They just conferred with each other for a minute. Then they listed the rules.

Pretend you don't recognize anyone, they said, even customers that come in often. Wear sunglasses to hide your eyes. Keep your hands out of sight as much as possible. Ask three simple questions. How long would you like your room? What is your preferred method of payment? Can you see the elevator, down the hall to the left?

I spent the rest of the afternoon walking. I followed the water a while. I watched the city's glow transition from day into night. At ten, I was back, ringing the doorbell, waving to the woman through the glass. She buzzed me in and showed me everything I needed to know. She introduced me to the guard in case anyone stayed over their time. She reminded me a custodian came around two.

Did you forget your sunglasses? she asked.

No, I said, I've got them.

She left me there and customers trickled in. They all waited patiently, quietly, as I fumbled with credit cards and selected keys. One woman asked if I was new, and I didn't even nod. How long would you like your room? I answered. What's your preferred method of payment?

I got the hang of it quickly, and a month passed in routine before I realized I had no idea what the crying rooms looked like, no idea what was going on above my head. I stood and sat down. I stood and sat down again. When the guard passed through the lobby, I asked if he'd watch the desk while I used the restroom. He dropped happily into my chair. I went down the hall.

On the third floor, I slipped a key I'd brought into its lock. I opened one of the doors.

I'd expected padding for some reason. I'd expected straitjackets and no furniture. What I saw was a simple family room. Twelve feet by twelve feet, a well-worn couch and a rocking chair with an afghan folded over the back. A rug covered much of the floor. Two side tables had coasters. A coatrack stood empty as if guarding something. On top of a sideboard slumped an antique radio.

I smelled lilac, chemical from an air freshener.

Okay, I said out loud. I turned to leave, but stopped. I heard crying, faint at first, then louder the more I became aware of it. I crept to one side of the room and then the other. I stood in the middle and craned my neck. I lowered myself to the rug, pressed an ear against it.

The crying seeped through two neighboring walls and the ceiling. It filled the air and mixed. I fell back on the couch like I'd been shoved. I took my sunglasses off and closed my eyes. I held my breath and listened, listened.

SOME CRYING SOUNDS like laughing at first. Some sounds exactly like it should. Some is wet, a blubber, and some dry as a dry throat. Some crying bursts in waves, like thunderstorms on a distant planet. And sometimes it stops, just stops, suddenly, a gasping, a choking and a gasping, before it starts up again. Some crying is jagged, like a comb. Some rises and falls like symphonies, like civilizations. Some sends jitters into the arms and hands and fingernails until they're scratching at the wall, at the floor, scraping and scraping the skin. There is heavy crying, light. There are notes in staccato, in moans. Some carry whimpers. Some shrieks and howls. Some full and upright screams. There is the crying that comes from the depths. Hundreds of thousands of years in the making. Crying that comes from among the echoes of coyotes and caves. And there is crying punctuated by words. Why and Why and Why, and O God and O God and O God.

THE NIGHT IT happened, I told my husband and son I'd be home for dinner. As usual, I pulled into the driveway hours late.

I'd expected every window to be blazing. My husband moving from room to room. My son finishing his homework. Two or three TVs on with nobody watching. But at nine thirty, the house was dark. I got out of the car thinking they'd gone to the movies, though they rarely did that. Inside, I smelled no evidence of cooking, so I assumed they'd eaten out, though they didn't do that much either. And when the dog didn't shuffle to greet me, I thought maybe they'd taken her for a walk.

I left all the lights off until I got to the kitchen.

There weren't any dirty dishes in the sink. No books or notebooks open on the table. No abandoned pencils on the floor. I wasn't concerned, not yet. I was happy to have the house to myself for a minute after all those extra hours of complications and surgery.

I thought, One of my son's friends must have had a birthday party. Or maybe my son had remembered something he needed for class and they'd rushed out to get it.

At ten thirty, I texted my husband as I ate a bowl of cereal. I called twice, three times, four. The silence began to wrap. Quieter than usual. Quieter even than when I sometimes woke in late morning, my husband already at work, my son at school.

I thought, Wherever they are, it must be crowded. Wherever they are, they must not be able to hear.

At eleven, I decided this was their attempt to punish me. I grinned at that. I laughed my own angry laugh.

I began turning on every light in the house. The dining room and living room. The theater my husband and son had set up for video games and movies. In the basement, I flipped every switch. On the second floor, I lit the hallway, the chandelier. I turned on lights in our bedroom, in my office and my husband's. Even the lamps we never used. Even the ones with bulbs covered in dust.

At my son's door, I shivered. I'd promised never to go in without his permission, but I turned the handle anyway. I switched on his light.

THERE WERE RULES meant for the protection of the place. Rules meant for the protection of those who came in. Customers were not allowed to share rooms. Not even couples or family members or friends. No children under twelve. Before people went up, they put their phones in a Ziploc bag and gave the bag to me and I kept them locked up until they came down again.

I sat behind the desk for a second month, like a knight behind his shield and armor. I learned to speak from the top of my throat, each word growing softer as it traveled along the palate toward my teeth. I was used to slack faces at the hospital. Dull eyes. Lids that, when open, might as well be shut. I knew blue lips. I knew fingers not quite willing to touch. I knew distances that came on, the dementias of shock.

But here, pain expanded and swelled with all the qualities of a haunt. I joked to myself that time lurched at the crying rooms only when I turned my back or only when I didn't see it crawling underneath the furniture.

I imagined my son in the lobby. Darkness folding outside the glass behind him. The sidewalk streetlamp yellow. Winter limping. I pictured the dog, curled. My husband sometimes filling the other armchair, his feet without shoes, his feet up on the coffee table.

I studied the customers through my glasses, admiring the way they had to make their grief public in front of me before taking it back into private again. One woman introduced herself every time, always asked my name. She booked her room in eight-hour blocks and sometimes twenty-four, and she ate at the restaurant across the street, framed by the window, peering out.

I don't mind letting you know, she said one night. I've got all the money I can spend and nothing to spend it on and no real will.

I don't mind letting you know, she said on another. Sadness is very close to nothing. It is so much like nothing at all.

She always wore sweaters that were too big. Sweaters that covered her much too much. It took all her energy to smile, so she rarely did.

I'll tell you, she said, what I come to cry about. If you want to know.

I do, I said before I could stop myself, but I don't, but I shouldn't.

That's about right, she said. That's about right, isn't it?

I took her phone and gave her a key. As soon as the night guard came around, I asked if he'd watch the desk.

I was in the habit of going up to the rooms almost every night now, and I'd even started arranging customers around one I'd keep open for myself in the middle. My heart beat faster on the stairs, my lungs almost burning. And inside, it was like listening to an orchestra warming up. The instruments unaware of the others until every once in a while they locked into place. Harmony like magic. Magic like someone yawning in a crowd and everyone else yawning too, one by one, in strings.

I let out the breath I'd been holding. I checked my eyes for wetness of my own.

SOME CRYING IS just a tear down the cheek. Some a churning, a far-off emptiness, a stare. Some is like vomiting, a purge. Some is weightless, a body flipping, a body flailing, a body falling toward rocks. There is the crying of babies and children. Of desperation and need. There is the crying of confession, of salvation, of guilt. There is crying that takes the place of the unimaginable, the uncomfortable, the inconceivable. The crying that follows death into its darkness and pitch. Some is so clearly the crying of loss. Some is so clearly the crying of those who have lost. Tears blur the words of an unfinished letter. Tears lead like a path into sleep. Tears, unmoored from gravity, flow upward and outward in dreams. Some crying cannot be clamped or caged. With some, the chest warps and strains, the mind seals, plugs. Strength disappears, arms and legs. The stomach tries to stop it. Then the throat. Then the muscles of the chin hold like a dam, fighting until they can't, fighting until they have to give way.

IN MY SON'S room that night, only his shoes and my husband's, side by side. In the center of the carpet. The police saw no evidence of a struggle or anything to indicate my family had packed and left. Nobody came forward to say they'd seen them. Nobody called demanding ransom.

Bodies streamed into the hospital as they always did. Bodies in all manner of shape and damage. I imagined my husband and son in the place of each. Bloodless, on the floor, the dog between them, it's four legs kinked and splayed. I imagined myself poking a finger into their wounds to test the depth. And my finger kept going. Deeper, deeper. Like I'd dropped a pebble into a well and was waiting for the splash and would never hear it.

I hired a private detective. I spent months searching on my own. I lost myself in the Internet and read and read. I believed in aliens for a time. In multiverses. In ghost ships and gods and airplanes vanishing in the sky.

I blamed my son. I had to. I thought, It must be his doing.

Premonitions dissolved. Suspicions led nowhere. I woke, heart racing in the empty house and empty bed. My thoughts splintered, and I grabbed at them, yanked them back. A pain began between my ribs, the pinpoint of stress spreading outward.

One of the boy's teachers told me he was the quietest student she'd ever had. He paid attention, but he hadn't said a thing all year. She didn't know what his voice sounded like. Couldn't even guess.

He was quiet at home, I said, but not like that.

It was hard not to see a shell he built around himself, she said. And in that shell, it was hard not to see a threat.

He was a teenager, I said. He was supposed to be angry.

The other kids liked him, the teacher said. I got that impression. I liked him too.

She told me they'd started sending my son to a therapist. Three periods a week. She was meant to help those who fell behind or those who had trouble grasping language or those who needed work to strengthen the right muscles. My husband had okayed it but hadn't said anything to me. My son hadn't either.

At my husband's firm, the other partners agreed he'd been a fantastic lawyer. They could tell he was a fantastic father, too, all those photos framed on his desk. The private detective found my husband had had three emotional affairs. But he hadn't seen any of the women in years, hadn't emailed, or spoken to them.

I'd always thought of myself as not easily rattled, but I finally had to admit I'd been shaken.

Had they deserved it? I asked. Had I? Could I have saved them? Can I still?

When the answers all seemed to be no, all seemed to be staying that way, I took a leave from work. I asked a neighbor to check the house once a week. I locked the door and left and wasn't sure if I'd ever come back.

THE city had restaurants on every block, thousands of them. The one across the street was the type where candles flickered over white tablecloths. They'd pasted Chinese letters above the door. Hung photographs of gondolas and cathedrals, temples and the Taj Mahal.

There was no rule against eating there, and I began to go before my shifts. I often saw the woman alone at her table near the window. And one night, when we arrived at the same time, she asked if I wanted to join her. She asked again the next night, her voice unsure, rehearsed. The night after that, she sent a waiter.

I finally gave in. At her table, I told her that sometimes I didn't even order anything.

I'm not hungry either, she said. I only ever feel like I should eat.

I wasn't wearing my sunglasses and we made eye contact. In the candlelight, I could see her gathering her courage.

I just work there, I said. I'm not some kind of priest.

The waiter hovered and the woman spoke to him in a language I couldn't quite identify.

I might have ordered too much, she said. You can take whatever's left.

We stared out the window. People hustled by with their collars pulled up to cover their faces and necks and chins. The snow couldn't stop them. Couldn't slow the city down.

You said you wanted to hear, the woman asked. Do you still?

She smiled, pained. My daughter, she said. My daughter died, and I can't get over it. Everyone gave up on me. Everyone else has left.

Was she sick? I asked.

The woman shook her head. It was my fault, she said. It might have been.

We looked out the window again until the food came, and then we ate almost everything, passing dishes back and forth.

I checked the time and put my glasses on. I have to go, I said.

The woman crossed the street a half-hour later. How long would you like your room? I asked. What's your preferred method of payment?

An hour, she said. Only an hour tonight.

I swiped her card and gave her a key and marked the time. I took her phone. I locked it up.

The hour dragged as usual. Stretched like that moment between death and announcing the time of death. Tubes all lifeless. Wires. The monitor startled and humming.

When the woman didn't come back, I assumed she'd fallen asleep. I pressed the button for the bell in her room, rang it twice, three times, four. I was supposed to call the night guard, give him the number, and he was supposed to knock and check.

Instead, I pocketed two keys and waited for him to come around. I asked him to watch the desk.

Someone had painted the metal bannister in the stairwell the same color as the cinderblock walls. The paint had bubbled and warted like skin. I forgot and touched it every time. I pulled my hand away every time.

On the fifth floor, I let myself into the room next to the woman's. I heard crying under my feet and to my left, but nothing on the right. I left the room and stepped back into the hallway. I went to her door. I cupped my hands against it. I shivered at the silence. I slid the key into the lock.

Inside, I saw an empty couch and chair. The yellow of the woman's coat hanging from the coatrack in the corner. I thought, She must be in someone else's room. Then I thought, She's gone too. She's disappeared.

I felt a push against the door. The woman behind it. Her laugh a true laugh, a real one.

I was standing against the wall, she said. Listening to you ring. Trying to get myself to leave.

She studied me.

Sit down a minute, she said.

She closed the door and locked it and led me to the couch. I took my sunglasses off and we sat there, side by side.

Do you ever imagine your daughter in here? I asked.

Yes, the woman said, of course.

Does she ever speak? Does she ever tell you where she is?

The woman didn't answer, and the two of us studied the wall like we might suddenly see beyond it. A customer wept in another room. One howled. One said, Why me, Why not me.

We should have made this impossible by now, I said. None of this should be possible anymore.

The woman touched her fingers to my back. Light, so light. I put by head on her shoulder.

SOME CRYING TURNS like a hurricane, some falls in a patter, some hovers as mist. Some crying stalks the house in silence, pretending not to notice. Some lays dormant, ticking, a bomb. Some dismantles the horizon. There is crying that can only come in new cities. There is crying of anger, of unhappiness, of remorse. Some crying is like being behind a curtain or being behind a world behind a curtain. Some ferries like a vessel or a ship, at the mercy of weather and wind. Some is fragile, on the edge, threatening to break until it does, a stone through glass, a sheet of ice on the sidewalk. There is crying of tragedy, of shame. There are snivels and yowls and caterwauls. And some crying sutures. Some stitches, some staples and binds. Some replaces, transplants, transforms. And some crying is the best way to get to blood, the best way to get to what lingers. Some is like seeing, almost. Some like understanding, almost. And some is like accepting, almost, what can't be, what won't be, what isn't and what is.

HADARA BAR-NADAV

The Blind

I was the deep reader of dirt.
Deep reader of the cracks in black shoes,
      heels worn down at an angle.
Deep reader of toy trains and dust.
Nightmares became my sticky friends soaked
      in honey like the corpse of a dun-haired boy—
all shine, even in death.
Deep reader of wildflowers whose seeds I crush
      into the soil with my boots—
five-finger, creeper, bindweed, bloodroot,
jimsonweed that made the teenage girls go blind for a day,
and jewelweed because we are all jewels and weeds,
      also known as touch-me-nots,
though the hummingbird arrives and dives in,
trembling the scene, viridian blur, thrust and entry,
troughs of her bone tongue, insistent needle-beak,
feasting on a golden universe I will never see.

SHANGYANG FANG

Which Are Almost, Which Are Not

Whatever he sees in this world he sees as words—

this kleenex, flown in the syntax of a magnolia,

is bundled into a swan. Not the swan itself,

nevertheless, more comprehensible. Scentless

pistils slit the planet open in the perennial cold

light of sun that fills this blue tabulae, mortal

as a meadow, through which he drifts. After all

the reality becomes penetrable. After all this world,

where words are warped substantial, stretching

their slim fingers to fulfill him, fails him. For he

knows despite knowing all things, he the sheer noun

is known by none. He the kernel of noumenon.

This feeling clings to his heart, eternal as a metal.

Maybe it is time to forgo. He moves by unmoving,

in which way whatever once belonged to him

drifts away, himself away, whatever was made

crooked is smoothed, the knotted neck of kleenex

swan—none shall know what it had once become.

DAVID KEPLINGER

During Snow

In an elevator during a snowstorm, a small crowd is thinking about snow. They don't see the snow, there are no windows, it's a very small elevator in France, in Paris, typical gate guarding their hands from the floors they watch rising past them. They are descending like snow, toward snow. They don't hear any snow, the negative sound of the snow, how it pulls down with it some redundant hum there is no name for. But they are thinking of it, they believe it will bury them. . . . *Je déteste la neige*, a woman who survived the war, thistle-like and crooked, announces to no one, between the third and second floor. Even as a few of them laugh, as they fall faster than the snow can fall, the woman keeps her head stiff-straight, her eyes ahead, dead serious.

Time

The cinema, that rainy day, was warm and dry. Its film was silent. A horse was racing with a Model T among our stiff black coats and hats. The car puffed smoke. The white horse snorted. Then the film stopped. The crouching horseman had fallen half out of frame. Only in stillness like that, my friends, will God and Devil call the truce. Then it started up again, as if letting out a breath.

TROY JOLLIMORE

Marvelous Things without Number

After forty or so summers you kind of get
the idea: the slow deepening of the plum-blue dusk
that offers a backdrop for the stately silhouettes
of disconsolate, sentinel-like telephone poles;
the fading chorus of evening birdsong; the sharp hollow
pong of an aluminum bat making contact
with the ball somewhere off in the distance followed by
the joyful and at the same time somehow mildly
forlorn minor uproar of a clutch of children cheering;
eventless days at the beach, the scorched sand
stinging beneath your feet, the sand in
your clothes and your hair, a relentless ubiquitous
grit that remains undislodged after any
number of showers and shampooings; the familiar
dirt that collects underneath your fingernails
and your hair growing longer; careless
afternoons endured and discharged in the backyard
hammock or a languid folding chair by the lake,
reading Amy Clampitt, reading Rilke;
teenagers playing an eternal game
of Monopoly or Risk that might well be
the very same game they started last summer;
the same hummingbirds taking the same flight paths
back to endless empty abundance
of the same backyard flowers and feeders . . .
Some friends are renewing their vows, they were married
a decade ago. Some friends are driving
up to one of the casinos on Friday
to hear a tribute band who have modeled themselves
after Led Zeppelin or Journey.
A friend who left for the East Coast two years
ago has flown back to Chico to take photos
of Mount Lassen exactly one hundred years after

its catastrophic eruption. For a while
it feels as if everything is a reenactment
of something that has already happened: even dumping
a skitter of Raisin Bran into a bowl
and then pouring milk over it, or sitting
on the porch or trying on sneakers takes on
the aura of a ritual. Are you trying
to deny time and change, to say that death
will have no authority here, or are you
celebrating the fact that everything is
in flux and ungraspable, or is the season
doing one or the other of these things for you?
Mornings glow like dreams, like memories, with
a radiance that has been lying latent
in the earth all night, you can do it again
(whatever *it* is) but you know that you can't do it over:
the beautiful girl, kissed, can't be unkissed
(and who would want that anyway? But
you might), and so you repeat, repeat, repeat,
feeling rich with existence and time
and a kind of exhaustion you have learned to savor;
the end of Side B, after all, simply means
that you flip the record over and listen
to Side A again. And did you say that life
would always be this way, or were you told that
by someone in the past, and now hang on to that belief
in the face of what must be mounting but, for now,
still invisible evidence to the contrary?
Stay invisible, you say to it, stay, you whisper,
stay just as you are, just a little bit longer,
which is just another way of telling the story
you tell the children every night, how the birds
and the rivers remembered the songs even when
the people forgot, and how, when the people
regained the ability to remember,
they learned the songs again from the birds
and the rivers. The children's wide, trusting eyes
as you say this, as if what you said was, to use
that phrase we used to like to use, the gospel truth.
It's only a story, after all. You mean

no harm. No one means any harm. The world
is ancient, full of shades and spirits, not all of them
friendly, and we do with it what we can.

SASHA BURSHTEYN

K[yie]v Spring

Every season is one season to Lyudmila.
Pollen pills the air. Night fades down. Lyudmila's mind

whistles down its regular rails.

On TV the same three men,
one doctor, one chemist, one lost to time,
promise in static to the populace.

Don't worry. Don't drink
the water—drink red wine. Red wine
vanishes from the shelves.

Lilacs bloom. The stations clog
with women, clutching their children, boarding
every train, any train, as long as the direction is

away. Lyudmila sends her children away.
Lyudmila stays.

Lyudmila comes home from work,
in Kyiv, then Kiev, and showers, and showers,
and showers. For months,

she tastes metal in the air.

On TV, on loop, a helicopter breaks
apart, mid-air, in grainy black
and white and gray. Cracks

into pieces. As smoothly as if someone tugged on a string
that runs along the seams
of the world.

It stays with me all night. All
night I run the fingers of my heart along the seams
of my body—throat, lungs, breasts, knees, collar-

bones. By the time Chernobyl crashed, her husband
had been dead ten years. Now the town
is home to bison and wolves. Like any disaster,

it has its tourists.

LESLEY WHEELER

Uncanny Activisms

> We light the poem and breathe out
>   the growing flames. Ahi kā. This
>   is our home—our fire. Hot tongues out
>
> —pūkana—turn words to steam. This
>   fish heart is a great lake on a
>   skillet. Ahi kā! Ahi kā!
>
>   from "Ahi Kā—The House of Ngā Puhi," by Robert Sullivan

"CAN SAYING MAKE IT SO?" asks J. L. Austin in *How To Do Things with Words*, a study of the social power of language. Saying means doing in many everyday situations, but that doesn't mean poetic declarations are bound to exert real-world effects. It makes a big difference, for instance, whether I'm reading these words silently on a Virginia campus, listening to an air conditioner whine, or Robert Sullivan is reciting them on Pacific land. Even commands by the president of a wealthy, well-armed county—such as U.S. Executive Order 13767, entitled Border Security and Immigration Enforcement Improvements—do not ensure that a wall will rise.

The sentence "I claim this land"—one way of paraphrasing Sullivan's "Ahi Kā"—may, under certain limited circumstances, possess contractual force. Think of King James granting a charter to the London Company to found a colony between the 34th and 41st parallels of North America, regardless of the nations already established there. A declaration may also exert incomplete force, or no force at all, unless accepted conventions govern its utterance and all persons involved participate deliberately in a ritual social exchange, intending to follow through on the contract's implications.

Whatever the real-world circumstances, according to Austin, a speech-act such as "I claim this land," or "We grant your request for asylum," sounds "hollow and void" in the inherently fictive situation of a poem: "Language in such circumstances is in special ways—intelligibly—used not seriously, but in ways *parasitic* upon its normal use . . ." Austin didn't regard poems as performative utterances. Yet poems have long imitated prayers, spells, curses, and charms, and this poetic mode seems to be proliferating. Its practitioners can be quite serious about making verbal patterns with power to change everything.

•

Keep the fire. The sun's rays are ropes
    held down by Māui's brothers.
        They handed down ray by burning

ray to each other every
    day—we keep the home fires burning
        every day. Mountains of our

house are its pillars—I believe
    in the forces that raised them here.
        Ahi kā burnt onto summits

char in the land, ahi kā dream,
    long bright cloud brilliant homeland.

THE SOCIAL CIRCUMSTANCES of Sullivan's prayer-poem "Ahi Kā" include ongoing disagreements about land rights in Aotearoa New Zealand. Sullivan is a writer of mixed ancestry—the biography on the back of the 2005 collection in which "Ahi Kā" appears, *Voice Carried My Family,* identifies his "Ngā Puhi, Kāi Tahu, and Irish descent"—and his work frequently explores the implications of this heritage. Ngā Puhi, the "house" of the title, refers to a Māori iwi located in Aotearoa's Northland region, iwi being variously translated as people, nation, or tribe. These iwi played a historic role at a defining moment in Aotearoan history. In 1840, Ngā Puhi chiefs signed the Treaty of Waitangi, a founding document of New Zealand as a nation, but what the treaty meant then and means now is vigorously contested, particularly its implications for sovereignty. Words won't transform discord into peace if the people involved don't agree on their import.

Sullivan's poetry conjures the living presence of history and the continuity of an indigenous worldview, even though he composes primarily in the colonial language. Every published version of "Ahi Kā" I can find—in *Voice Carried My Family*, the multi-authored chapbook *Shade House,* the anthology *Mauri Ola,* and online—gestures to potential readerships by including glosses of Māori vocabulary and custom. For *Best New Zealand Poems 2005,* for instance, Sullivan explains:

"Ahi Kā" refers to the practice of keeping the home fires warm. It is a cultural symbol of maintaining your presence on the land. The mountain pillars in the poem refer to the district of the Northland tribe Ngā Puhi which is likened to a sacred house or shelter. For those who might not know, a 'pūkana' is a fierce facial contortion often seen in haka.

I wrote this poem overseas—it is my way of keeping my heart close to home.

Sullivan slips between worlds here, assuming some references are familiar while elucidating others. "For those who might not know" gestures toward a tentative, speculative community. He defines "pūkana" but not "haka," the dance famously borrowed by the All Blacks. These details project an audience with information about New Zealand, but not necessary Māori, culture. In the back of *Voice Carried My Family*, slightly longer notes seem to anticipate a more ignorant international audience: Sullivan, for example, glosses "the culture-hero Māui," because while "Ahi Kā" responds to historical crisis, it is also religious. A culture hero can be historical, mythological, or both. The very term blurs realities, or perhaps insists those intellectual distinctions are beside the point.

The question I bring to this poem is a version of Austin's: does Sullivan's performance of his claim to place make it so? What meaningful differences exist among, for example, a treaty, a poem, and a ceremony? All seek transformation through language, but to varying degrees, they require social agreement to work. Finally, if any of those questions are answerable, are those conclusions transferrable? Under what conditions can a spiritual poem be activist?

•

Ahi kā our life, ahi kā

carried by the tribe's forever-story
        firing every lullaby.
                Shadows shrink in our hands' quiver

as we speak—ahi kā sing fire
        scoop embers in the childhood sun
                stare into molten shapes and see

people—building, sailing, farming—
        see them in the flames of our land
        see them in this forever light

POETRY AND PRAYER are kindred genres, acts of communication exercised in formal, public, communal rituals or in emotionally-charged privacy, perhaps with little hope of a direct answer. Prayers can be spontaneous outpourings or traditional texts passed down over centuries, comprised of incantatory lines permeated by repetition. Repetition, after all, links one prayer to a series of earlier professions of faith, emphasizing the persistence of spiritual traditions over long spans of time. Even for people estranged from such traditions, like me, repetition can induce a state of self-forgetful peace or ecstatic connection.

While "prayer" often designates a text, it's not just about words. Praying includes nonverbal behaviors—assuming a posture of supplication or moving in prescribed ways, such as the dancing Sullivan alludes to in the phrase "hands' quiver." Prayer is also a speech-act in that, to quote Austin again, "the issuing of the utterance is the performing of an action." The circuit of communication may not be complete by Austin's terms: individuals may feel God's answering presence, but there is no incontrovertible evidence confirming divine receipt of the message. Still, even if religious invocation doesn't change the weather or the course of a disease, there are social and personal effects. It affirms the existence of a faith community. Prayer may also transform the practitioner from within, bringing serenity or strengthening feelings of religious commitment.

Maybe my devotion to poetry represents a sad, debased deflection of religious impulse. I read literature desperately and teach it with ardor, but beyond campuses, conferences, and reading series, my spiritual practice tends to be lonelier than churchgoing. Yet so many poets, skeptics, and believers, and everything in between, channel the transformative magic of prayers, spells, charms, curses, and blessings: a few on my reading list lately are Kazim Ali, Niall Campbell, Danielle Legros Georges, Jennifer Givhan, Joy Harjo, and Jane Satterfield. Rhythm and repetition contribute to enchantment. Metaphor—the rhetorical device by which some theorists define poetry—ignites a verbal metamorphosis. Mountains become the pillars of a house. A poem becomes a fire.

·

        no tears only fire for ahi
            kā no weeping only hāngi pits
                no regrets just forgiveness and

OCEANIA, THE *BIOGEOGRAPHIC* region uniting New Zealand, Australia, and many other countries and cultures, is defined by connections across water rather than confined by the populations of specific islands. Robert Sullivan is therefore both departing from home when he takes a job at the University of Hawai'i and "retracing migration routes . . . *return[ing] to* an originary home," as Alice Te Punga Somerville writes in *Once Were Pacific*. Māori and indigenous Hawai'ians share many traditions; across the Pacific, languages and beliefs resemble one another closely. One example offered during my New Zealand Fulbright orientation in 2011 was the concept of "taboo"—*tabu* in Fijian, *kapu* in Hawai'ian, *tapu* in te reo Māori. James Cook first introduced the word to Europeans while describing Tongans' refusal to eat or drink in a sacred place.

Tapu is both religious and legal, because these concepts are not separate. Hence Sullivan's poetic assertion of "ahi kā" is both a prayer and the fulfillment of a contract. The iwi's communal land-rights accrue from occupation signified by the kindling and maintenance of home-fires as well as other practices: building sacred structures; singing *karakia* to honor the spirits of the earth, air, and water, who are also revered ancestors; learning what plants grow there and what birds dwell in the forest. All of these behaviors confer *mana whenua*, meaning the power or right of guardianship over the land.

"I believe," Sullivan declares, nourishing that fire the only way he can from a distance of four and a half thousand miles. First-person-plural pronouns outnumber that lone "I" by nine to one. By praying through the relatively private genre of lyric poetry, Sullivan negotiates between personal and public devotion, but the prevalence of the pronouns "we" and "our" emphasizes the ceremony's ultimate status as a communal declaration. A similar balancing act governs form and syntax. While "Ahi Kā" is dominated by present tense verbs, its arrangement into triplets links past, present, and future. Striking enjambments over lines and even stanzas enact culture's continuity, despite all the forces ranged against it.

While conditioned by the context of Sullivan's residence in Hawai'i at that moment—he was a man at home, yet far from his customary lands—"Ahi Kā" seems to aspire to timelessness. Written in the westernmost part of the United States, the poem asserts a continuing presence on a spur of Aotearoa's North Island. And while existing primarily in print and attributed to a single author, it invokes not only song and ceremony but alchemical metamorphosis, as if burning up the paper that carries it to readers.

"Ahi Kā" may or may not satisfy the ancestors. As the Treaty of Waitangi demonstrated, paper is a fallen and untrustworthy medium, and translation can lead to deception or at least profound misunderstanding. Nevertheless, it transforms the speaker from a displaced person into a keeper of old laws. A reader is also transformed by encountering it, although perhaps only in tiny ways. A memory is created. Emotions stir. Sometimes a reader's attention is captured more completely; you spend a few minutes entranced, in flow, losing time as if stepping out of this world for a moment.

A poem's ability to evoke such an alternate possible universe is, paradoxically, linked to its proximity to nonliterary genres such as prayer or legal contract. In *Poetry and its Others,* Jahan Ramazani calls this nearness "intergeneric dialogue" or "a dialogic poetics," noting how poets highlight the vitality and distinctiveness of their own genre by assimilating and transforming other kinds of discourse. By peering over the edge, you understand where you live. Yet there is more to the effect than juxtaposition. Alluding to legal customs, song, dance, religious chant, and other traditions that structure our relationship to one another, Sullivan reminds us that poetry constitutes instrumental communication as well as a more private zone of linguistic play for its own sake. Poetry is potentially saying and doing. By invoking a virtual world and acting out rituals there, one might even nurture right relations between human beings in their everyday lives, and between people and a living earth.

"Ahi Kā" conjures a scene with its first words and invites you in: "We light the poem." Perhaps I am especially ready to step across the limen, because I smell smoke. This bit of land is a house roped to heaven. It is also a skillet and a dream and a cloud. Metaphorical transformations help us know the territory more vividly.

Any imaginative person can stare into clouds or flames and envision animals or landscapes; poems inspire similar illusions. Sullivan drives this point home by including, in his fire-poem evoking a faraway place, people staring into a fire and glimpsing that very faraway place. When you "sing fire" you can "stare into molten shapes and see // people—building, sailing, farming— / see them in the flames of our land / see them in this forever light." This is the House of Ngā Puhi as it was, is, and will be, members of the iwi inhabiting customary lands by right of ahi kā. The stanza break after "see" inserts a pregnant delay, that moment of release as one crosses from one reality to another, but the visionary world trumps the everyday one, because it is "forever." Different times collapse in the poem's liminal zone.

It's not that experiences of spatial and temporal unity are impossible in ordinary life. Anyone can "meet" Sullivan online, through a variety of websites. I search for his name and distances fold as I remember my own trips to Auckland and his subsequent visit to my campus. Look, now he's teaching at the Manukau Institute of Technology, near Auckland, New Zealand's largest city. I can imagine his voice thrumming through the digital texts I find. ("You know," he said, eyeing the twilit colonnade that houses my office, "this place is haunted.")

Semi-magical technology isn't even required, when it comes to feeling how past and future inhere in the everyday present (or recognizing, from either side, what powerful, instrumental fictions borders can be). I worked on this essay in a country in crisis, on a campus named partly after a commander of the Confederate States Army in the U.S. Civil War, a conflict that still agitates people around here. While I parsed linebreaks, I thought about refugees housed in miserable conditions and whether I could help them, beyond donations to immigrant legal services. While I riffled through *How To Do Things with Words,* I thought about enslaved human beings of whom my university once claimed ownership, whose labor, and whose subsequent sale to a Mississippi plantation, enable my air-conditioned parasitism. Paper wills, lists, and bills of sale—

and the social agreements honoring these words—transformed people into money. It can be hard to believe in such a brutal magic from my comfortable distance, but it remains urgent news.

Those enslaved people and their stories are gone, memorialized by fragile legal documents transcribed in sepia-colored longhand. It is also true that slavery is forever, that it never stops happening here and now. That the two-point-five square miles of Lexington, Virginia, a tiny fraction of which I hold the deed to, are also Monacan land, though traces of Monacan occupation are even harder to see now than the vestiges of slavery.

I'm not sure anyone can make a persuasive claim to being fully *here* if they won't admit the flicker of forever light. Poetry helps carry it. It isn't enough to spend time in those alternate possible worlds—other words must be spoken in other fora. Yet political activism by conventional means isn't enough, either.

> a place for the fire—it's our song
>   to sing—ahi kā—got to keep
>   singing the shadows away—ha!

Translation Folio

LUCAS HIRSCH

Translator's Introduction

Donna Spruijt-Metz

I MOVED TO THE NETHERLANDS, ostensibly for a year, to study classical flute. I ended up staying for 22 years, and Dutch poetry was what helped me learn the language and navigate the unexpected culture shock. When I wanted to share some of my favorite poems with my mother, I had to translate Hans Lodeizen for her, because he wasn't (and still isn't) widely translated. I loved the work of it, the piecing together of language and meaning, the careful weaving between sounds and cultures. When I moved back to the U.S., I continued to translate Dutch poems to English, to read Dutch poetry, and to try to keep up a bit with new Dutch poets. I had, however, never worked with a living poet, and that was something that I really longed to do. I wanted to be able to ask if I had gotten it "right," to work as a team, to go back and forth with a piece of poetry together.

I met Lucas Hirsch in July of 2018, and was immediately taken with his work, perhaps because he is inspired by many of the poets that I admire—Lucebert, Hugo Claus, Gerrit Kouwenaar, poets who made up the movement in The Netherlands known as *de Vijftigers* ("Those of the fifties"). According to *de Vijftigers*, truly vital art could only be made by truly free people, and the esthetic conventions of the time hampered artistic freedom. In particular, their emphasis moved from formal characteristics such as rhyme and meter towards greater syntactic freedom and more associative leaps in order to cultivate spontaneity. These values deeply resonate in Lucas' work. I was honored when he asked me to have a go at translating a few of his poems.

This cycle of ten poems, "Devil's Fair," is the result of our first collaboration. It combines all the various poetics that Lucas has played with throughout his last four books. With this new work, he has produced a poetics that is spontaneous and direct, clearly inspired by *de Vijftigers*, as well as by Allen Ginsberg and the Beat Generation. However, Lucas pushes the boundaries, placing his unique voice clearly in the 21st century. The poem cycle uses informal syntax teeming with Dutch vernacular. This makes for beautiful and surprising poetry in Dutch. It also makes these poems extremely difficult to translate into English. The countless slang expressions and Dutch aphorisms rely on understanding the current Dutch culture and political climate, on knowledge of Dutch food, social structure, and climate. Although I have deep ties to the Netherlands and visit at least once a year, I haven't lived in there for a few decades. The slang and colloquialisms therefore presented an extra challenge.

The process of translating "Devil's Fair" was a team endeavor, rich and informative and often playful. My best friend in the Netherlands, Caecilia de Hoog, is a translator. She translates novels from English to Dutch, which is an entirely different business than translating poetry from Dutch to English. But because the colloquialisms were so difficult, I asked her if she would mind having a look at my first translation of the first poem in the cycle. She ended up looking at all of them. She was a great first eye, and before I sent anything to Lucas, she gave it a once over. I am deeply indebted to her. After I incorporated any edits from Caecilia, Lucas and I began the process of going back and forth. For each poem, Lucas and I went back and forth several times—six to seven times for some of them. He would comment, I would make changes (or stick stubbornly to my guns), he would see what he thought of my changes (or stick stubbornly to his guns), and so it would go until we were both happy with the results. And then we sent it off to *Copper Nickel.* The poem cycle is part of a full-length manuscript, *Wu Wei Eet Een* (*Wu-Wei Eats an Egg*), which is coming out in Dutch in February of 2020. We are now at work translating the full manuscript.

LUCAS HIRSCH : A Poem

Devil's Fair[1]

1.

The morning we buried Father the heavens threw a Devil's Fair
Along the approach to the funeral home, cherry blossoms shimmered
in the watery light. The roof of the limousine that brought us to the entrance
thrummed in syncopation. A hedge of umbrellas stood waiting
beyond the widow and we got into the mood. The crowd was made of many
while we were made of burden. We bore a past
and bent, as rain does trees, the time

2.

The sun peeked through branches that covered a few heads, caressed women's shivering
pantyhoesed legs and the slick black paint of car hoods and
doors slammed shut with dull thuds
It was a grumbling commotion. It was an animal-like gathering
The hearse's lift gate stood up like a watchful dog's tail
It pointed towards He who had taken Father
The wet black nose was aimed at its prey: the waiting, drenched attendees
Everything imploded, narrowed, seemed to change its mind
Sound was the gravel adding our feet to the crowd
Sight was the light landing on what was to come
When Dad was unloaded an honor guard formed
Who or what was honored was a mystery to me
So was the location that was chosen for the eulogy
The undertaker called it one of Rietveld's architectural wonders
and had it dragged from a forgotten corner of the country to a
vacated piece of land along Schiphol's fifth runway where

---

1. "Devil's fair" is a Dutch colloquialism for what Americans sometimes call a "sun shower"—i.e., when it rains while the sun is out.

the boxy white building would lend some panache
to the dead and the living
His enthusiasm had been catching

3.

At the reception we took off our best coats and stepped
into the foyer a size smaller. *Music for Airports*, by Brian Eno,
was playing. Father had asked for that specifically before he
was lured into death, a different person. So he wouldn't die
too heavy the cancer had fed on the scraps of his heart for ten days
I could see his ribs and I thought under them it all had broken apart, sunk
and shrunk to his core. Where had he gone, given the level of opium
that had wandered through his body, was an odd question
but I allowed it. I saw an opportunity to calculate how long
a meager life lasts. After all, a person must go somewhere
with their questions for death

4.

As if it is perfectly normal to die when
humanity is sleeping, you passed away. We felt sick
and we blamed the timing and not death for our sorrow
With a sea of flowers splashed along the aisle and over your casket
you lay there. They provided comfort and a pleasant smell. Our eyes scanned
the attendees. They nodded when we made eye contact. They stared, spoke,
sympathized with each other when we weren't looking. Humanity in all its glory,
humanity in all its anxiety. It gave us perspective

5.

In the distance, a Boeing took off and I thought there he goes again on the way
to somewhere else. Even now he needed to escape. To land
where he could forget home. The women, the money, the booze and grandeur
before he got sick we complained about it. Now that he was dead
we wished him safe travels. The tide had to turn eventually. That he had to die

was likely the reason that we cried but decided to be strong and
think of our new lives without him

6.

After we listened to a number of old friends, Miles played a few notes—
an antidote. If you give them the chance, men of a certain age will fill their surroundings
with childish bravado. Demand attention. Only their swallowing
between words betrays their desperation. The number of "I's"
that filled the speakers' throats revealed their level of fear
Talking about yourself keeps you from dying. There are many ways
to exorcise death

7.

Bruce Springsteen's *The Ghost of Tom Joad* rippled out of the speakers and
then it was up to us to say something. But what do you say if you already said
goodbye days ago and have calculated the exact last point at which you were all
together? Do you say that he is dead and once was Father? Perhaps a friend?
Do you say because he found peace he will never sit next to you on the couch again
and have a conversation about which you will think *whatever, can you
tone it down a bit?* Each of us gasped for words,
crushed out a few sentences, looked at our paper, looked up and fell silent
Of course there was an aunt with a poem:

*I find the song that fell out of your jacket pocket / I use it to stanch
the bleeding / I fold it into a swallow / Then I fold an
anchor / and finally fold your full heart / You must know that I won't forget you /
even as I let go of your hands*

She looked as if she expected to lift off the ground but didn't do it
Instead she tried to make eye contact, thus creating little moments
with each of us. She nodded as she read
I stared through the auditorium to the outside surroundings
drawn from thin air. A bottomless pit
in which I saw a bit of space. It shone with life

8.

After the last number it fell to Mother
to deliver the final blow to her life with Pa. The mouth that opened
was economical. The words that were chosen to make sense of him were meager
We murmured a prayer and followed Father to the grave lying in wait for him
a short ride up the road in the clammy cold weather of duty
I thought I recognized my marriage in all this and my heart sank

9.

We all stood looking into a freshly dug pit. A straight-sided
death-box we could fit into but we didn't fall. We held our ground
by standing in a circle around the hole. To break with the straightforwardness of life
Everything shuddered in the rain. Everything dripped, bent and broke. That was it
Goodbye man, goodbye Pa, goodbye friend and enemy. Thanks for coming
Food and drinks were served at Pa's favorite cafe. They knew what he liked

10.

Once we'd eaten and were back home it was time for reflection
This threw silence into the struggle. In which my wife and I aimed arrows
at each other living in the house as two spirits
Hearts moved like cloud cover sometimes opening sometimes closing
I was moody and I asked my wife for her forecast
A few months later she answered our marriage
was finished. Dried out shriveled where once it was fertile
The rest was decomposing underwater and washed away
She was the flood and I was oil on the fire
She had a Devil's Fair to dispel and I chose to leave

—translated from the Dutch by Donna Spruijt-Metz

MAUREEN LANGLOSS

Here, Take My Hand

TWENTY PEOPLE ENTERED A BLACK, windowless box—ceiling on high, apples in bowls, props against walls. One small boy brought a pile of leaves—golds and oranges and other crunchy colors—and jumped in and out, in and out of five girls playing a game on a board, shaking the hourglass till it shattered, summer sand running through fingers onto the boots of three teenage boys searching for exit—wings shut, crossover jammed—clutching binoculars, eyes tilted up up up above young lovers, all tongue and hand and want, hot and probing, sighing, bumping, burning, rolling end over end over three women cradling spring air, inverting glass bottles at the altar on stage left, warm milk dripping down down down on two middle-aged friends in overalls by a woodblock, raising an axe and dropping it, raising an axe and dropping it, raising an axe and on and on and on beside an old couple cutting memories from photographs—college football games, a winter wedding, rooks in flight—handing shears back and forth. Back and forth, I recorded them all with various devices—typewriter, black box, lie detector, felt tip pen—a riot of truth and untruth, of stretch and fail, of kindness and spite, of love and love and love, in in in until the last man made a ladder of us a hundred feet tall to a skylight that appeared when we climbed then pulled, climbed then pulled, one after the other after the other.

Raised Rising Risen

Spring. And I feel like winter. Sitting on a park bench dedicated "To Mort, even though he was an asshole." I watch a woman with something stuck in her hair push a stroller. Something white like a cotton ball, a tampon, a tissue. Hair so wild, so stiff with life. I once had that lifey hair.

Tampon or tissue, either one—a crisis. A cry for help. I wish I hadn't made Nicole cry. My best friend. I should have never called her self-absorbed. I've spent thirty-five years not calling her self-absorbed. Though, it was true, she never asked after Lucy, barely acknowledged she existed, not even when she was a newborn. Rarely asked how I was. How I am now—with Lucy raised rising risen. When I most want her to ask.

Spring and the wind is too fast and this young mom walks too slow. She blocks the people on the path behind her rushing rushing. They pass her, zoom zoom, to the C train to the Starbucks to the SoulCycle. They don't notice, don't want to notice, the crisis tissue tampon in her hair, the way each step is a mountain to be scaled. I want to bring the tissue to my skin, wipe away this chill, this vanity of a friend who tells me again and again what she thinks, what she wants, what she's doing doing doing.

Nicole never had a child of her own. Spring and I am winter and suddenly the young mom stops. She parks the stroller and people pile up behind her. They bump, crash. Stub toes. They excuse the young mom anything, everything. They smile at her, nod their heads. Middle aged friends, however, lifelong friends, won't let the smallest thing go. A single compound word.

Self-absorbed. I open my canvas bag. Nothing inside but a few saltines in plastic in case I get hungry watching the young moms, the people living lives. I gave this bag to Nicole for her fiftieth, filled it with bath salts, journals, honey glow wrinkle cream. It has a picture of a lighthouse rising from the mist and says you are my beacon. After the compound word, she gave the bag back, along with everything I'd ever given her. The half-a-heart necklace. How did she still have it? I'd lost the other half decades ago. It doesn't break her heart not to have a child, she says sometimes. She never wanted one anyway.

Spring and my teeth chatter and this young mom bends over a patch of orange tulips. A dreamsicle orange. She strokes the cheek of a single flower.

I don't believe Mort was an asshole. People just never looked beneath the surface, couldn't be bothered to find his humanity. His sluggish, tarnished humanity.

The young mom hesitates, pulls her hand back from the tulip. She looks up to the blue sky—sky so blue I hate it I love it—as if asking permission. Light washes over her face and she plucks the flower, separates bloom from stalk, sets petal on palm.

Fire in a dish. The mother's face glows with delight so naked I have to turn away. I'm naked too.

Spring and I feel like February, caught without a coat, without a Lucy. I watch as the naked mom brings the tulip to her baby's face. Look, she says, look, my love. It's a flower. She brings the petals close closer to his eyes. The love could burn them. F-L-O-W-E-R, she says again, placing it under his nose. He inhales deeply, and I inhale too. There beneath the color: a citrus scent that couldn't possibly be true. The first navel orange I fed to Lucy, the pucker in her baby smile, the peel unraveling to the grass. I shiver as the mother glides the baby's hand across the tulip's skin. Feel, she says. Her delight is his delight and mine and the blue blue sky's and I want to tell Nicole and Lucy and all the fire flowers I love you love you love you, but before I say it out loud, a woman stops short beside our tulip patch. Her dark hair pulled tight behind her ears, her glasses too small for her face. I touch the rim of my own bifocals. Are mine too small? As the woman taps the mom on the shoulder, her skirt rises above her knee.

"How dare you pick the flowers! It's against the law. This is Central Park." Her pronunciation is exact. Seething.

"I'm sorry," the mom says, blushing under her wild hair.

The flower drops into the baby's hand.

"Other people might want to enjoy that tulip. Did you think about them? When another child passes, he won't get to see that flower because your child saw it all."

The baby makes a fist around the tulip and squeezes tight. A slice of orange peeks out from between his thumb and finger. The woman yells and the child cries. Am I crying too?

There is a great gust, a shower of snowflake petals. I rise from Mort's bench with Nicole's bag—cherry blossoms falling inside it. I approach the woman with glasses too small to see, to look deep into the eyes of an orange that ignites in the hand of a young mother, in the nose of a baby boy, in me. I rush at her, still not sure what I will do. Why will I do it? I raise my foot to the creases that have formed by the bending of her knees, over and over, through a life. I push, hard harder against them until the knee wilts. I stand over her, a blizzard of heat. I raise my bag above my head and let it fall. I strike her, blossoms erupting from my bag. How could she be so selfish? Removing the tissue from the young mother's hair—it's a tissue after all—I wipe our tears, say "There, there. Where does it hurt?"

Montauk

I.

Josh found his mother crouched on the floor across the room from her suitcase—an open-mouthed beast in vinyl she'd received as a wedding gift in the 1960s. She'd never used it, and now it was making a messy meal of her blouses and medical devices. Heating pad for crumbling vertebrae, nebulizer for lungs.

"I'm not going," she said over the rattling of her own body.

Josh repacked her. Lucas had called this a fool's errand. Lucas and his clichés and his pessimism annoyed Josh. But maybe he was right. Josh took all the things out of the suitcase that his mother wouldn't need: Ziploc bags containing photographs he'd published, acceptance letters from nursing schools she'd never attended, prayers on index cards. *O my God, I am heartily sorry for having offended Thee.* He removed his father's last wallet—a scrap of paper with Josh's old cell number inside. His dad had never dialed it, had only spoken to him in clipped sentences since Josh first brought Lucas home from Montauk. To think, he'd been excited to introduce them, giddy even. He'd had so much hope that his parents would love Lucas too.

Now he carefully folded each piece of clothing like his mother had taught him when she'd sent him off to college thirty years ago. Cross-country via Amtrak by himself.

"This is a lot of sweaters, Mom. Can you pick just one?"

His mother retreated into the hug of the drapes—which stood at attention, ready to fend off the dawn. Josh chose the sky-blue sweater, because his mother always looked happy in blue, even if she wasn't. She rarely was. When the suitcase was ready, his mother refused to rise. He put his hands under her arms to help her to her feet, but she went boneless like a child. He scooped her up, and she grasped at the long hair of his beard.

"I'm doing this for you," he said.

Carrying her to the car, he was surprised how light she was compared to her suitcase.

II.

The windshield wipers stopped working an hour from home. Josh got out of the car in a driving rain. He wished Lucas had come. Lucas was the one in their relationship who could repair what broke. Your mother doesn't want me there, he'd said. She and

Lucas had a lot in common—love of the evening news and black licorice and animals that others found ugly—but she still didn't know it. Josh wondered if they should turn back. What was the point anymore?

Eventually, he got one wiper going. One was enough.

His mother checked her seatbelt, made sure the window was closed. She looked behind them as they got farther and farther from the Illinois border, from her flat town of single-story homes near the Caterpillar factory. He'd made a playlist of songs by decade he thought she might like, but the rain was so noisy they couldn't hear unless he turned it up too loud. The feedback in her hearing aids was terrible. Instead, he told her about dipping his hand in the surf in Montauk—how much better that water was than any other water. It could change a person. He described the glaciers and deserts he'd photographed for work. The oyster Lucas had pulled from the coast of Chiloé and shucked for him with a key. If she was listening, he couldn't tell. It had always been like that between them.

"You're going to love the ocean," he said when they stopped overnight in a roadside motel outside Harrisburg.

III.

IT was late afternoon when they arrived to the end of Long Island. Josh steered the car head-on into the sand, setting the water before his mother like a painting on an easel. Pretty streaks of pink pierced the cloud-cover, but the water itself was a muddy blue. He wished it were bluer. He felt angry at the ocean for not looking its best at a time like this. When he'd met Lucas on this exact beach twenty years before, the water had been the kind of blue that makes a person fall in love.

Josh removed his mother's shoes and rolled up her pants.

"You can't half-fill a suitcase, Josh," she said, smoothing a crease on her knee. "If you leave empty space, everything shifts around. The clothes get wrinkled."

"You're right. I'm sorry."

The sand was hard for her to walk on, so he held her around the waist in case she stumbled. She did, but only once. Refusing the chair he unfolded for her, she walked down the gentle slope to the shore alone—her steps steadier on the packed, wet sand. When the cold blue touched her toes, she didn't recoil the way most people do. She walked straight into the autumn waves until they crashed up to her shins, tugging her back and forth like a reed that had always been there, that already knew this life. His mother stayed planted in the water a long time, taking deep, salty breaths as the contents of the Atlantic rushed toward her and away from her, toward her and away. The litter and krill and shipwreck. Someone else's memories. Her son's memories. Josh concentrated on the swirls of sea foam at their feet so he wouldn't cry. At dusk, his mother took a Ziploc from the pocket of her sweater, filled it with sea, and asked him to take her home.

"Lucas's eyes are the color of that ocean," was the only thing she said on the long drive west across Long Island.

LEIGH ANNE COUCH

Overbite, 1969

Go away, baby. I want to see the cars, the shoes,
the late-sixties Southern-spiffy clothes, the parents
and grandparents, the bully uncle, the aunt who must
be pregnant with Gary the way the camera lingers
on her stomach, but then your head with three teeth
(yes, count them) fills frame after frame.
Flap your little hand so we can move on
to the grandfather before he loses that slick grace
and most of his speech to a stroke one morning
while eating canned biscuits, and to the mod grandmother
in black polka dots who still works at Penney's
before the stroke when she won't leave
the house some days because she can't
fasten her bra across the welts on her back.
Oh my god, it's Christmas! and the baby adores
her new green rocker. The other grandfather,
the nice one, loves to watch Pup-Pup lick the baby
from toe to forehead. The waves of laughter from this
happy happy baby are soundless. Go back to the teen
boys who look like runners at an ad agency
and never once ham it up for the camera.
The only sullen look caught on film
is from the bully uncle's son who grows up
to bully his mother. Most of all I want
to see the father and the mother and the father
with the mother—but someone has to hold the camera,
someone has to make the money, make
the dinner, take care of the baby, blow
off steam, see a man about a dog. The father
is so thin and with a lovely overbite
but the camera was his idea and his regard
for the baby of course, for old ladies caught
unaware, and for houses: Colonial, ranch,

Spanish, front doors, patios, even under-
construction, any house not his own,
he luxuriates in hypothetical lives.
The father is thin and, with a lovely overbite,
his smile is more like a grimace for the camera
or for the mother holding the camera for once.
The mother loves Peter Pan collars, cat-eye
glasses, and that baby, how the mother loves her,
and how the baby loves the mother's soft clean skin.
But the baby is just a baby acting the way
any baby would, so why this hitch in my throat
when the father reaches for her? I whisper
to the mute screen, to myself, *reach back,*
reach back, don't make him sad so soon.

KELLY MORSE

Origin Myth

If you ever need to remember
the name of Artemis and Apollo's mother,
if you feel guilty for only ever answering *Zeus*
as parent to all heroes and minor gods

(his children's mothers fly-sized erasures)
as if his calf-slip incubator equaled a uterus,
remember the golden twins' mother, Leto,
by remembering Jared Leto, either

in his current troubling iteration
playing a trans woman and declaring
her creature (as if centaur, satyr),
another man transforming woman to beast—

or you can instead remember Leto
in the plum-fleshed silence of Jordan Catalano
no doubt as Zeus remembers his bride, all eyes
and a body built for potential, calfskin

projector screen stretched under the skin
of a gaze. Lately there seems to be a resurgence
of *Friends*, my students appear sunken in
oversized white tee shirts with each letter connected

by dots, denotation of the simplest kind.
How can there be any real desire for Ross,
a broom in the closet and who needs it
except to clean up a mess, like Rachel aging.

Friends' problems dissolved like sugar on the tongue
which is why I categorically reject it
in favor of *My So Called Life*
where parents had affairs and got divorced and went bankrupt

and gay kids sometimes got beat up and had nowhere to go,
the line between virginity and not
palpable emptiness between nose ring and nose.
Claire Dane's chin had its own starring role:

before the tears came the wobble, we'd kneel
before that pixelated rashy flesh,
sense the grotesque tripwired in our faces.
Yet we pledged allegiance to Angela Chase

because then maybe we ourselves were desirable
and not just to Brian Krackow
(a Hephaestus if there ever was one)
but to the fair-limbed Catalano, doe-eyed lunk

as befuddled in the meadow of his own beauty
as we were, surrounded by tear gas mist of teenage angst
that made us want to retch—Catalano had a mask
but followed airplane adage of saving oneself first, offered

his beautiful-yet-without-additional-gas-masks hands, clouded
as Zeus often was, leaving bounty hunter Hera to chase
progeny birthed in caves, out of eggs and golden showers,
and somewhere a woman with a volatile chin was crying.

JIM RICHARDS

The Big League

When Emily Dickinson wandered onto the baseball field mid-game, play stopped, but no one chased her as they chase a streaking fan—perhaps because she wasn't running or wasn't naked. Her angle took her past first base toward center field and her gaze was fixed on something far away. *She wants to pick that dandelion,* shouted a know-it-all who cheered for the other team. But there were no dandelions in the freshly mown field. *Shut it you nimrod,* came the reply. A fight ensued, and things were seen that are rarely seen without a fight: a chili dog entered a falling man's armpit; a t-shirt was stretched to the length of a skirt; a bead from a broken necklace landed in a cup of beer. Emily slowly made her way to the other side as people were distracted with more pressing spectacles, but in her wake she left a strange and memorable violence, a slap of the mind followed by a slant echo in the heart. Soon enough the fools were escorted out of the stadium, and the long and boring game resumed.

Hotel Management

When I stopped worrying about beauty so many possibilities appeared. I wrapped a white plastic knife, spoon, and fork in a white paper napkin, and sealed it in plastic. I didn't need to explain it anymore. I was content to wipe my feet on a worn-out welcome mat. I stopped charging my tenants for leaving their mirrors on at night. If I needed art, I could hang a rag on the wall and frame it. (Please clean your hair out of the sink.) But beauty is different than confusion—it tries to creep back in. I look over my shoulder when I'm sitting at the front desk and see myself looking over my shoulder. (This uniform has a stain, that one doesn't.) I need to hire someone new for the night shift. Are you interested?

JENNY BROWNE

Javelina, Javelina

We should know more of the history
of the historian, so to better understand
the version being placed before us

but javelina might not see it this way
as they don't see so well at all
though their back teeth clack in warning

when they smell the dogs, *my* dogs, all four
sprinting up & over Pinto Canyon Road,
so in no particular order then I, historian

of this poem recall a vertebrae practicing
minor scales in the shade, the taste of salt
on a sleeping man's wrist, one star called

back home by a different name each night,
someone whispering *Uno*, a blue rinse
to the sharp Chisos & even myself

aging carefully as a one-armed cartwheel
between the yucca all that spring
& if what I really wanted was to show you

the instant we saw the javelina
seeing us & wondered if we were safe
you may wonder which of the living

left gasping on the southern edge
of borrowed earth where barely runs
a collapsed lung of a river we mean by *we?*

Even history might hesitate, if it could.
The javelina prove to be more interested
in the action over at the quail feeder

& sky in the liquid sound quail make
rising all at once, a sound like shaking
the eulogy it took you all night to write

but you mean to say all your life
even if we don't recognize our own
bared teeth & scarf of grizzled black hair,

grief staring back from the ridge, arriving
as it can, so many years after the fact.
Do we still imagine our experience

to be unique? Think of the first known photograph
of a human taken on an empty Paris street in 1838
although the street was in fact packed

with bodies in motion. Now I'm talking
to you, my dead, who held so still, being
both all I could & could not see.

EMILY BLAIR

According to a Recent Study, Rats Experience Regret

They look back over their shoulders at a cherry-flavored reward. They look back over their shoulders at the laboratory door. Sometimes they wake up wondering about the system. They rue our similarities as warm-blooded mammals with the same basic body plans and goals like home ownership. They lament our differences in lifespan and institutional support. Like us, they have meta-cognition, and know what they don't know, like where the resting platform is in the water maze or why a group of rats should be called a mischief and a group of humans a committee. Wild rats carry disease and shame, can tread water for three days or fall fifty feet and survive. They have bigger hearts. One liked to stop by and sort the recycling bin in my kitchen, faint clanking barely discernible over the waves of my white noise machine. When I turned the machine off, the rat would stop, waiting for the return of the sound of surf we both found so soothing. Another rat once had a winter picnic inside the hood of my parked car, leaving the engine littered with chicken bones. Neither of us could think of one good reason not to move to California. Then there's the rat I saw last night, swinging on a water pipe like a trapeze artist, straight into my open basement window. Probably with a crazy laugh. Outside a lab, there's no way to be sure, since rat laughter is ultrasonic.

CHRISTINA BEASLEY

Domesticated

At last, the sea pig: vacuum cleaner of the ocean floor.
When Martha described her request to her mother,
it was the final proclamation on a fairly empty Christmas list.
Her family sought to oblige: they could not afford a Dyson.
Churchill claimed pigs were our equals in earlier speeches.

The teacup type was "in," anyway. Tiny pigs taught young ladies
to be dainty sophisticates. Adorned with bonnets, they shared
a slew of human skin diseases. Relatable, social, they could eat
anything. Surely one around the homestead would prove valuable.
She was confident her parents would make these assumptions.

Aquatic pigs use water cavities to inflate their tube-like feet,
but Martha knew this. They exhibit a strong desire for rich,
organic food. They travel in trawls of 300 to 600. They are
elongated, congealed slime tubes. Sea pigs are not good
on a leash because sea pigs do not have eyes. They wallow
in all of the puddles. Procuring them is a great challenge.

Martha loved her sea pig more than anything. She taught it tricks,
like absorbing the detritus of an entire whale corpse in the span
of a month. Its name was Abe, short for abyssal plain. Slave to no one,
it only cleaned when hungry. It seldom gossiped, it was the silent type.
It did not need to please. These qualities were respected and admired.
Martha learned to be formidable through the company she kept.

To halve and to hold

A group of desperate children is often referred to as a murder.
They shuffle back and forth, sniffling inward, flexing their palms.
The death throes of the sliced earthworm are strangely entrancing.
There is not a dry eye on the playground.

They have only named and gendered him after realizing the pain
they have caused. Horace. Horace claimed he did not know
how to dance or entertain a crowd. The murder is regretful
to see this proven false under such circumstances.

Horace nudges the dirt with what we assume is his head.
He is embarrassed. He sighs a tiny earthworm sigh and lolls
against clover and clod. I stand to the side, supervising the rawness
of nature and recess. I am reminded of my ongoing divorce.

After much dismay, another girl is heavy with silver lining.
She explains they have turned one Horace into two.
In attempting to dig a tunnel to India, they have produced life.
A catastrophe like this can transform mortal into god.

In truth, worms are lucky if even one half survives dismemberment.
They do not have a second stomach brain waiting for its age of primacy.
Two cannot be made from one. I want to describe conservation of energy,
but the same notion keeps me from speaking. I blink wearily.

I am grateful. I only have one heart to ache from bisection,
and not three; although Horace may now only have two.
The minutes tick onward; a bell rings. The mathematics falter and slip.
I ask the murderer to cut away half of my heart, which is so swollen and sad.

They oblige, using the cafeteria arsenal of small plastic knives
and hand soap from the restroom. The operation takes three hours,
all next to the swing set. The muscles eke apart like sweaty fruit.
They stretch tendrils amongst themselves. I remember a soft sort
of singing. Everyone overjoyed. The grass pulsing beneath my calves.

Adaptation

In threatening times, the lyrebird mimics
the songs of modern predators.
Creatures unmoved by cats and foxes.
Trills the emphatic yelp of car alarms,
continuous chuckle of camera shutters,
low, discordant rumble of chainsaws.
Trucks lumber across the fields, fat and
bellowing as buffalo; photographers cackle,
omnipresent, hawkish. Loggers' tools
gnash teeth bared all at once.

The lyrebird has lived as it does
for fifteen million years. Master
of the forest masquerade. The lyrebird
fluctuates rapidly between replicating
what is desired and what is unwanted.
It thrives on presentation, feathers
splayed out like open palms.

It is unafraid of mislaying its who
and endlessly guided by its why.
The art of imitation is the art of survival.
We are not sure what remains, or why,
but whatever it is keeps on singing.

LYLE MAY

Learning to Die

UNIT THREE'S PODS REMINDED ME of the Buncombe County Jail cell blocks: L-shaped twelve cell tiers, bright fluorescent lights that banish shadows, white walls and steel tables amidst a light grey painted dayroom floor. Except this was death row and red lacquered paint coats the doors, rails and stairs. Compared to the old death row blocks on Unit Two, Unit Three's pods were sterile, capacious, and vermin-free when they opened in June of 2002.

Nearly two hundred death row prisoners moved to Unit Three, and I knew a few dozen, mostly from the two blocks I had lived on before our exodus. The rest I heard about, saw once or twice, or did not know at all. When I arrived on the row in March '99, I did not have much opportunity to interact with people from other blocks. In the old building the only chance we had to intermingle between blocks occurred at Bible Study, and not many willingly suffered through an hour of Biblical excoriation just to hang out. Unit Three's pods, four each on the two floors, sat adjacent to one another so we could wave through giant Plexiglass windows, shout through cracks in the hallway doors, or stand in the hallway and talk when the pod doors opened for chow and outside recreation.

Assigned to Pod Eight, I only knew about half of the guys there. Settling in proved easy enough because getting to know people in prison is only hard if you have never been there. Once in prison you can get a feel for who you might be able to talk with and who should be avoided. It remains something of a process though, a tricky dance reminiscent of high school, but more dangerous.

When I met Eddie, he sat hunched over a dayroom table playing a card game my mother taught me as a child. From what I observed, Eddie seemed quiet and mild-mannered. No signs of sudden psychoticism or cruelty. No frothing at the mouth or telling twitches. For all intents and purposes he appeared a normal middle-aged, pasty-faced white guy with a perpetual three day beard. He didn't talk much or loudly—loud mouths, braggarts, and know-it-alls are the bane of every prison cell block in America. Mainly, Eddie looked forlorn.

"You play cribbage?" he asked and gathered the cards. In jail and prison, playing cards or other table-top games has less to do with leisure and more to do with a shared medium through which people can communicate without any awkwardness or discomfort. Engaging in a game—any game—also gives people a chance to discover your character, and provides you an opportunity to learn about others.

I hesitated before sitting. I didn't know this guy, and despite needing to learn more about who lived around me, caution was always necessary. Was he a predator? A bully? Or worse, somebody who would draw people like that? In my first few months on the row, I had to prove to others I would not be punked or bullied. Young white boys have it hard in prison if they lack a will to not only defend themselves, but live free of any future harassment. Thoughts of my first fight on death row ran through my mind: An older black man named Fly tried to push me around, verbally disrespecting and otherwise letting me know what he thought of white people. When I asked him to cut it out he said, "Whatcha gonna do about it white boy." So we fought and I earned my respect.

Eddie quickly dealt the cards as I set pegs in the cribbage board. Rules of the game returned with memories of rainy summers playing cards in a tent my siblings and I set up in the backyard. While we played, Eddie asked where I lived before becoming incarcerated. "Maine," I said, and his eyes widened a bit. "And I regret ever leaving."

"Maine? No shit? I should've stayed in Newport News or Virginia Beach."

"Hey! I've been to Virginia Beach. I took a Greyhound there in November of '96 thinking it would be crowded. The place was deserted."

"Yeah. You should've gone in August or earlier. The nightlife is amazing." We spoke knowing it had less to do with where we missed and more to do with a shared desire to be free from prison and the threat of execution.

Over the next few months Eddie told me he worked in a pawn shop and about the different things people from all walks of life sold there. I soon discovered the pawn shop stood central in Eddie's life. Whenever Dan, Tim, JJ or I sat with Eddie at chow he would find a way to interject, "That reminds me of this one time at the pawn shop," and immediately launch into a pawn shop story that lay on the shelf of his mind, marked at a discount: buy one, get three for free.

I always felt disadvantaged swapping stories about the outside. The amount of time I spent away from the sheltered world of my parents' house in Brunswick spanned three years. Between those ages of sixteen and nineteen my freedom was perforated by stints in a group home, rehab, hospital, and the Maine Youth Center. I knew more about life inside institutions than life on the outside. So I listened to certain older men like Harvey, Mule, Earl, and Roper to rid myself of any naïveté. They stood in as uncles and mentors in a place with few role models. Eddie was more of a peer, so his stories about selling everything he owned as cocaine and alcohol consumed his life were relatable.

"Man, I stayed high and drunk every day," he said. "Three and four day binges where I couldn't even remember my name or where I put my car. When I started shooting cocaine it was over. I'd wake up in a different zip code, in a strange house, struggling to remember anything." I nodded, glancing at the TV, overcome with kinship and discomfort because of the similarities to my own drug-hazed journey to death row. Beyond a shared addiction, Eddie and I held no expectations of each other aside from a quiet conversation about a book, movie, or song on the radio. Our conversations, like those of others I called "friend," were devoid of the posturing and lies typical in prison. And, of course, we discussed the executions.

In December of '02 Ernest Basden and Desmond Carter were put to death. Questions about Basden's innocence helped him get a few stays but they were not enough to save him. Unit Three's atmosphere stayed the same as it had in the old building during an execution; tense, brittle, and oppressively quiet, as if too much noise would break loose a scream of terror trapped in all of us. We suspected the state would make up for the low number of executions in 2002; we were right. 2003 became the deadliest year for death row prisoners since North Carolina reinstated the death penalty in 1977.

An execution is scheduled by the warden 90 days in advance of the date, but the condemned are almost always notified 45 days into that period, after the Court, attorneys, and state receive notice. The condemned is summoned to the warden's office, informed an execution date has been set, and asked if he or she needs anyone contacted. About once a week, until the final 24 hours on death watch, the warden summons the condemned to his office – willing or not – to ask after his or her state of mind. Like the warden, check-ins with a shrink are mandatory because a condemned prisoner has nothing left to lose, making him a significant security risk in the eyes of prison officials.

By the end of July 2003, William Quentin Jones was scheduled to die August 22nd; Henry Hunt, September 12th; and Joseph Bates, September 26th. As their dates approached, Eddie grew increasingly distracted and nervous. When I asked about it he said, "I'm out of appeals and I think I'm next." I didn't pay it much attention because Mule's date drew nearer and Eddie seemed uncertain, as if he was guessing and had received no official word from his attorneys.

Henry Hunt, or "Mule" as most of us knew him, was a good friend who taught me a lot. A full blooded Tuscaroran Indian from Robeson County, Mule and I received Catholic confirmation together in 2000 when Bishop Gossman came to Central Prison for the ceremony. A devout Catholic, Mule also introduced me to the resident stray cats in the old building, showed me how to make potato wine, fix a radio, and a host of other things only somebody who grew up in the country and prison would know. He was serious and funny, generous and slightly wild. My favorite uncle in and out of prison, Mule liked teaching me things because I listened – especially when it came to "home remedies" and finessing limited resources in prison. After playing with the cats, I noticed I caught a ring worm on my shoulder. Worried, I told Mule about filling out a sick call, but he stopped me.

"Boy," he said, "don't you know ring worm comes from animals? What you gonna tell them people? 'I got worms in the shower'? Come here." He then took a rag, dipped it in bleach, and rubbed the infected spot until it burned. "If that don't fix it, fill out a sick call and tell 'em you been playin with a mouse. Leave my cats out of it." Surprisingly, the bleach worked, leaving a light, ring-shaped scar on my shoulder.

Though Mule lived on another block when they gave him a date, I saw him at Mass every Thursday and was present when Fr. Dan gave him viaticum – the last sacrament of a Christian. If Mule was worried, I never saw it. He seemed resigned to his fate, as if peace came with faith and understanding a new journey was about to begin.

A week before the state killed William Quentin Jones, a man I never met, Eddie received an October 3rd execution date.

"What are your lawyers saying?" I asked, but Eddie just sighed.

"You know. Same bullshit they tell everyone. Clemency is my last best chance." After Harvey Green tried to demonstrate rehabilitation through his Christian ministry in and out of prison, and Ronald Frye provided reams of documents detailing childhood abuse—was even the literal poster child for the DHHS—both were denied clemency and put to death. My faith in clemency died with Harvey and Ronald, but there was always a chance Eddie could get that golden ticket.

Mule's execution was a gut punch that left me numb and breathless, unable to think or know what to do. I tried to read but just stared at the page, waiting for the trapped feeling to pass. It never did. Since I lived on the pod with Joe Bates, seeing him withdraw as his time grew short was unnerving. Normally, Joe played poker, talked about sports, or religiously watched *The Young and the Restless*. All of that stopped after Mule's execution. Joe sat on his bunk flipping through magazines, stood at a narrow window looking at the sky, or leaned against the wall, arms folded, frowning at the TV. He spoke little in the final days, and then only in terse statements. When the death squad came for him, Joe gave out some hugs and handshakes and on his way out the door said, "All right. Y'all be easy."

The day before they took Eddie to death watch for the final 72 hours of his life, we sat in his cell smoking cigarettes. Smoke streamed through a rectangle of sunlight, thick and poisonous with things we avoided in idle conversation. His time on death watch would be spent visiting with attorneys, family, and friends, many of whom suddenly wanted to visit after years of silence. Eddie's time on death row had been harder than most since he rarely received visits or money for the canteen. What he had, he received from those of us kind enough to give it. People on the outside never give much thought about what prisoners do to get by, assuming meals provided at the chow hall are enough, but state food doesn't always relieve hunger and a little money for canteen goes a long way. Without access to a job Eddie went hungry for years.

I watched a curl of smoke roll up the cell wall and hit the ceiling as we sat in silence. Was it like this for all of the condemned? This awkward time when you wait for the state to repossess your body? "Can I tell you something, man?" He stared at the floor, hands on knees, his face slack and unshaven. "I'm scared. I don't want to die." He looked up. "Why does it have to be this way?"

How could I answer that, after seven people had been released from death row over the last nine months, their sentences reduced to life or less? Eddie was convicted and sentenced under the felony murder rule, the only difference between life and death, a robbery conviction with the murder. Hundreds of murder cases like his ended up with life sentences because the additional felony was dropped in exchange for a guilty plea. Eddie refused to plead guilty and received a death sentence for exercising his right to a jury trial.

My faith in God was not strong enough to share with Eddie. Besides, we all prayed for deliverance from this nightmare only to awaken the next day, our lives ground into the concrete until only dust remained. It failed to comfort me, so how could I comfort him? Doubt and an overwhelming sense of helplessness made it hard to speak. "I don't know, Eddie. It just is." In my heart a voice spat bitterness: our lot is based on luck of the draw.

When they came for Eddie, a sergeant pushed an empty hand cart onto the block; the warden, unit manager, and a shift captain walked in behind him. The brass represented a display of North Carolina's will that Eddie be put to death for the murder of Herman Larry Smith. Eddie put a white plastic property bag on the cart: old pictures and letters to be collected by whomever came to pick up his body.

One by one, guys went over and gave Eddie a hug, dap, or handshake, a few saying nothing, others a brief word of encouragement.

"Keep your head up, Eddie."

"All right my friend, I'm gonna miss you."

"Stay strong, my man."

When my turn came, I struggled to think of something profound and symbolic of our friendship, but words failed. "Take it easy. You're good people to me." I hugged him and turned away, not wanting to see him cry. Not wanting him to see me cry. The brass escorted him from the block and out of sight down the hallway.

North Carolina's lethal injection is a three drug cocktail that included sodium thiopental, which acts as an anesthetic, pancuronium bromide, a paralytic agent, and potassium chloride, which causes cardiac arrest. It has never been adequately explained why an overdose of some anesthetic is not an option. After the three drug cocktail was administered, it took Edward Ernest Hartman nearly an hour to die. His attorney and other witnesses reported seeing him gasp and jerk against the gurney straps, his eyes fluttering open and shut despite being "sedated and paralyzed." The prosecutor who attended the execution, who could have just as easily given Eddie a life sentence, declared, "Justice has been served."

The day after an execution is like having a hangover; your head throbs and stomach turns; laughter grates on every nerve and the light seems too bright. That people are genuinely supportive of this misery makes it worse, but the state proved their support by scheduling three more executions after Eddie; Joseph Timothy Keel, November 7th; John Daniels, November 14th; and Robbie J. Lyons, December 5th.

In the same period, four more prisoners had their death sentences overturned and were sentenced to life without parole. Reconciling the seeming randomness of who receives life and who is put to death is not something I have been able to do. In the meantime, I think about Mule, Harvey, Eddie, and all the rest who were executed. I try to overcome the bitterness, anger and despair—and fail. Their faces rise up and engulf my thoughts in the quiet moments, leaving me to wonder which one of my friends will be next.

Translation Folio

RUMA MODAK

Translator's Introduction

Shabnam Nadiya

RUMA MODAK BEGAN AS A young poet, is a stalwart in theater (over the last two decades she has written, directed and acted in at least twenty stage productions), and now writes fiction as well—her third short story collection came out in 2018. She has won awards for her pioneering role in theater (she and her husband, both theater activists, continue to play a seminal role in rejuvenating the local theater world in their region), as well as for her fiction.

She also happens to be that rare creature in the Bangladeshi literary sphere: someone whose creative life is centered away from Dhaka, the capital not only of the nation, but also assumed to be the hub of all significant creative output and activity. To this world, Modak brings a creative vision that is rooted in "outsider" sensibility—because she is a woman, because she is Hindu (a religious minority in a Muslim majority nation), and because she chooses to make her creative home in the periphery, rather than the center.

Modak prefers to tell the truth the Emily Dickinson way: aslant. In her essay "Tell It Slant" the poet Camille Dungy writes that "good poems weird the truth, rearrange it, re present it, cause us to re-envision the past, to rememory (to borrow Toni Morrison's word) our own history." Modak takes themes that aren't uncommon (a girl trying to figure out where and how she fits in the world of the boy she likes in this instance), adds a complication (it's an interfaith relationship) and then makes the situation a little more awry, layering on topics of shame, culture, dominance, etc.

In a recent interview, Modak spoke of how essential it is for the writer to be more than a "loyal commentator," arguing that storytelling must move beyond mere reportage. In this, she is one of a newer generation of Bangladeshi women writers, who have moved away from defining femaleness with victimhood; or perhaps a better way to state it is that they've not moved away (because in a highly patriarchal culture such as that of Bangladesh's, gender shapes destiny for many if not for most), but that they have moved beyond, that they have—finally—moved towards capturing the messiness of what it means to be a woman when one's sense of self is cut through with the realities of gender, faith, ethnicity, class.

This story is a bright example of being aslant—while the reader is lulled into considering cultural differences between two young people brought up in different faith traditions and also inhabiting a rural/urban divide, through a minor character's actions, she deftly inserts the larger question of what it means to exist as a minority woman in a world that is communal and patriarchal in how it dominates. The main character, an urban, educated woman, and the minor character are twisted reflections of each other. A tale that is about an intercultural romance becomes inextricably tied to the story of the violence that is routinely visited upon religious minorities in Bangladesh, because that is the reality that religious minorities exist within. But in Modak's world, this complicated, complex, untidy world, a single question gets explored from a multitude of angles: which one is a more embarrassing topic?

When I read this story the first time, I was left to ponder: how much story can a single story hold?

One of the delights of being a literary translator is the privilege of introducing writers to a different language readership for the first time; this story is the first time Ruma Modak has been translated into English. I have a sense that it won't be the last.

An Embarrassing Topic

THAT TIME THE VOTE HAPPENED. That time? Which time was that time? Well, why do they need to know all these dates and times anyway? Year after year goes by, they feel no need to make sure precisely when the elections will take place. But when the elections are close, the "candidates" visit the village more frequently, canvassers flock everywhere, and even though they don't really need to, they still know that voting day is coming up.

That time, on election day, they bathed early in the communal pond, decked themselves up in oils-*sindoor*-creams-powders and, with their toddlers in tow, queued up to cast their votes at *Temunia Government Primary School*. The men in one line, the women in another. When their toddlers thrashed about on the ground, bawling to be allowed to vote, they took them to the polling officers to get their thumbs inked and told them, "There, that's a vote." And, after buying them bags of chips from the near-by store, they left. Back home, the women turned their television sets on straightaway, and only then did they begin their cooking on the coal- and wood-fired stoves, and because it was election day, the television station broadcast movies and song numbers all day, and they watched until their lentils burned in the pots, but what could be done, after all, it wasn't every day that the television station showed movies and song numbers. The fathers of their children ate the burnt lentils while their eyes too remained glued to the screen. The day went well up to that point; the trouble began in the evening. Who knows who won the election, or who lost, but the young men raised a din as they entered the neighborhood and first they set fire to Montu's home, and then they smashed the black and white television set and the mango-wood kitchen safe at Gonsha's to smithereens, and then they grabbed Niyoti by the hair and, dragging her behind them, they clambered onto the stoop of the Radha Madhab temple and chopped off the deity's hair and split open its head as they hollered and whooped . . . the racket continued throughout the night.

(Although the connection between this topic and that other, embarrassing topic may seem irrelevant on the face of it, perhaps the reader will comprehend how relevant it is by the end of this story.)

MONA OVERHEARD THE conversation between the two unwittingly. She had not meant to eavesdrop. That she did, was just a coincidence. Mona wasn't supposed to be home when the maidservant Parbati was talking to the mistress of the house Rajlakkhi

Debi. Nishi, Duti and Mona had gone out earlier to visit the Christian Mission that stood within walking distance of the house. Built during the British era, the Mission boasted superb architecture. Mona had left Nishi and Duti and hurried back, cutting her visit short, because she really needed to go to the bathroom. But neither Parbati nor Rajlakkhi Debi knew that. Mona was sure that if they had known she could hear them, they wouldn't have discussed the issue at that moment. No, her certainty didn't bank on the traits of the residents of this still-unfamiliar household. Instead it relied on the fact that the topic of their conversation was so embarrassing, common sense dictated that no one would have the poor taste to have Mona overhear the discussion.

She had met the inhabitants of this household for the first time just two days ago; except for one person. That one person was the thread that had pulled her to this house and its denizens.

Parbati was leaving no gaps in her attempts to explain to the octogenarian Rajlakkhi Debi just how deep ran the relationship between Mona and that one person. Which is why, when Parbati was mixing truth and lies, adding a smudge of lewdness, Mona's face burned in that stifling room. From what she overheard, it hadn't seemed to her that Rajlakkhi Debi, the elderly matriarch of this household after whom the house itself was named, was encouraging Parbati with questions. But because she couldn't see her at that moment, Mona couldn't gauge her true reaction.

The girl Parbati was clever, truly clever. But her cleverness came with a provincial, indecent curiosity and unbearable garrulity. Mona had realized this as soon as she reached *Rajlakkhi* and tried to be as careful as possible in her behavior and her speech. She barely spoke directly or one-on-one to Shomeer. Even if she was chatting with others and he was there, she kept herself at a distance, at times more so than her friends Nishi or Duti. Even though she had yearned to listen to the song "On this moonlit night, everyone has gone to the forest" while sitting on the moonlight-drenched roof of Shomeer's centuries old home, she had curbed her desire. She curbed her longing to clasp Shomeer's hand and get her feet wet in the waterfall flowing right beside the house. Still, when Shomeer's sister-in-law showed up bearing fluffy *luchis* and milk-curd *dalna* for afternoon tea, and they were all so excited—"Look, look, these aren't your Aziz Market luchis, just see how soft and tasty they are! *Arrey*, these are the real deal! Those things that we eat at Aziz Market are clones, luchi clones!"—Shomeer had smiled with pursed lips and said, "Come on, eat! Think of this as your own house!" and placed more luchis on Mona's plate. Even if no one else noticed it, Mona didn't miss triumph overwhelm suspicion in Parbati's eyes at that moment. She even discussed it with Nishi and Duti. They pooh-poohed her. "Forget about her, an s-e-r-v-a-n-t! Why give her so much importance?" Mona hadn't wanted to grant her such importance. But the mysterious smile glued to her face, her darting gaze, her uninvited curiosity and sidling up too close—all of it seemed calculated.

There was no way to not grant her importance. At one point she even told Shomeer, "That maidservant of yours is too clever by half . . . "

Shomeer took the chance to deliver a little jab. "What, you've already started complaining about your in-laws?"

Although the issue resolved itself in jokes for the moment, it didn't end there. Like scaling a mountain but stumbling on a lump of earth, her whole visit became complicated because of Parbati.

It would be inaccurate to say that Shomeer had told her just before they came here, rather it was from the very beginning of their relationship that he had given her an idea about the issue. It wasn't exactly conservatism. These were customs—rural, aristocratic Hindu families had to observe certain customs. Mona had prodded him. "*Eish*, now you're trying to lessen your culpability by labeling it aristocracy! Just call it what it is—conservative." Mona had known even before they had arrived that they couldn't tell his family about her relationship with Shomeer yet. Yes, she had had an inkling; but no matter what you called it, whether conservatism or orthodoxy, she hadn't been able to imagine just how deep and how far those roots spread.

If one didn't look for it though, those roots were hard to see from outside. Nishi and Duti hadn't. From outside, everything was neat and tidy. There was no lack in the hospitality or affection or sincerity offered to them. His family said, "Who knows what they feed these poor girls in those dorms!" And Shomeer's elder brother brought home a whole *khashi* goat, while his sister-in-law made *patishapta,* stuffed sweet crepes. His mother sent out for all the ingredients needed to make *hilsa* fish *polao.* But because of her relationship with Shomeer and her intense desire to take that relationship toward a conclusion, Mona's probing eyes had placed the atmosphere and the people of *Rajlakkhi* under scrutiny ever since her arrival. Father, mother, brother, sister-in-law, the various uncles and aunts, the cousins scattered all over Europe and America— Mona had tried to get to know them, had tried to get an idea, without letting anyone guess, just how unsuitable, or perhaps suitable, she was for Shomeer whose roots dug so deep here, in *Rajlakkhi.*

The closer and deeper Mona observed the place, the more dispirited she felt. Again and again, her love of three years lost itself in waves of indecision, hesitation, and diffidence. Although Shomeer had laughed it off. "Forget about it! Everything will turn out fine once we're married." What would turn out fine? The *pooja* platform was set out in the yard; every day the priest came to light the ghee-drenched wick of the five-flamed lamp to perform the *aarti;* the surroundings were permeated with the fragrance and fumes of incense; the women of *Rajlakkhi* sat in a long line spanning the veranda, even Parbati in a corner; and the other day when Mona stepped foot on the veranda every single one of them had shouted at her, even Shomeer—Mona had been mortified. If Mona entered this Hindu household as a daughter-in-law, would that situation change overnight? Would Mona be able to climb onto the veranda without hesitating? If her stepping foot on the veranda made them lose caste now, wouldn't their loss of caste continue to be a problem later?

After that experience, Mona's gaze became even more probing, searching for cracks. She noticed that the leftover food in the bowls that were so carefully arranged for them on the table never made it back to the kitchen. In the dying afternoon, Parbati tossed the leftovers into the pond, cleansed the plates and bowls, and bathed before she reentered the house. Mona still hadn't been able to figure out exactly where the kitchen was. Their comings and goings were limited to the two or three rooms in the outer part of the house. As if an invisible wall separated the rest of the rooms within the inner quarter. Rajlakkhi Debi herself never entered the room they were staying in; she stood outside and talked to them. No matter how many times they invited her, they had failed to get her to step foot in their room.

Neither Nishi nor Duti took Mona seriously when she mentioned these things. Instead, they had saddled her with the blame. "Oh my, just look at how sincere these people are! What's the point of stirring the pot looking for bad smells!" Mona couldn't quite explain her need to look for bad smells. Just as her relationship with Shomeer was entirely personal, the plan to take that relationship to a conclusion was also very much her own. So why not keep the need to stir the pot also to herself, if only to reach an understanding with herself?

But how could it remain private and personal after what happened today? Initially, Mona hadn't wanted to tell anyone. But when she couldn't find the things even after she looked, she was forced to tell Nishi and Duti. And, later, even Shomeer. She couldn't find either of the two pairs of panties she had brought with her.

Mona remembered quite clearly that she had spread them out to dry on the veranda clothesline and covered them with her blue scarf. She searched inside their room, the bathroom, their bags, the veranda, every nook and cranny, and finally, when she still couldn't find her panties, Mona had to tell them. Because they still had two more days here. The panties were an essential element of her urban habits, almost impossible to go without. She had no choice but to tell Shomeer; who knew where the shops or marketplaces were located in this small town that was more like a village? And now it was this act of telling Shomeer that Parbati was presenting to Rajlakkhi Debi as indisputable evidence of the relationship between the two of them. "Oh, *Didima*! Does a woman share such shameful talk with a man, unless he's her husband! I saw it with my own eyes, she was falling all over *Chhoto Dada*, touching him and whatnot as she told him about it!" Although she had gone on secret dates with Shomeer on campus, Mona hadn't spoken to him with any intimacy since their arrival here. She had been so careful and restrained, and now, listening to the prurience in Parbati's description, she felt so ashamed she wanted to hide.

When Shomeer's father returned from the market that evening, a huge meeting convened in the living area, with Shomeer at its center. Such meetings around the television set were regular events in this household. It was nothing out of the ordinary. But, unerringly, Mona observed the deep shadow darkening everyone's faces on this particular evening. Nishi and Duti were busy with Facebook, uploading photos from their morning's jaunt to the Christian Mission. It was pointless to try and explain it to them. These truly intimate, personal problems were never as important to others as they were to oneself. Mona noticed Shomeer was sitting there with his head bowed, as if he was at fault. It pricked her inside, more because of the issue itself than for Shomeer. So, among those comments and the rejoinders, none of which Mona could hear from over here, was the shameful topic of Mona's lost panties rearing up again and again? Perhaps not. But by now everyone must know that the reason behind this sudden change of atmosphere was that embarrassing topic. How humiliating!

The remaining time Mona spent at *Rajlakkhi* felt joyless, miserable, lifeless, unbearable. Apart from Shomeer's *Bou-di*, his sister-in-law, no one came outside to bid them farewell. As she walked them to the gate, *Bou-di* continued to sing that old song of what an aristocratic lineage her in-laws held, how they had preserved that pedigree and distinction through the generations. Because a daughter of this family had married a *Shudra*, a low-caste man, her father had invited guests over and held her funeral. Mona understood why she was telling them these stories at this moment.

As Shomeer walked them to the station, the dour expression on his usually radiant face seemed unfamiliar to her. In her head she tried to tally it up: just what kind of existential crisis would this family be plunged into by welcoming a Muslim girl as their daughter-in-law, just how would the fear of public disgrace break them? Shomeer was a sapling that had sprung from the deepest roots of their customs and traditions. No matter how irrational their orthodoxy, just how far could Shomeer be separated from it? And would that even be right? Without the joy of family, friends, celebrations, gatherings, what need was there to bind a person within the social ritual of "marriage"? How long could a person remain immersed in the infatuation of love—an emotion whose hidden truth was carnality. This conflict between her feelings for Shomeer and the culture she had just witnessed so closely distressed her. She placed her hand on Shomeer's and he covered it with his. He said, "You know, last night my mother clasped my feet and wept; she begged me not to destroy our beautiful family." Mona remained silent, while in Shomeer's tearful eyes, the shadows of devotion and distress could be read quite clearly. Overnight, an embarrassing topic had laid bare reality, had exposed the brutality of truth. A brutality that Mona had had no inkling of while attending the theater at the Shilpakala Academy or eating luchis at Aziz Super Market.

WHEN EVERYONE HAD left, utter silence descended all across the house. As if it was a neighborhood devastated by a sudden tornado. Rajlakkhi Debi paced from one room to another by herself. The guest room had just been scrubbed clean and tidied up. As she entered, she spotted Parbati examining something with her back towards the door. "What's that in your hands, eh? Show me, come on, show it!" Rajlakkhi Debi's voice contained a familiar displeasure. Parbati knew that although most people tolerated her habit of pilfering small things now and then, Rajlakkhi Debi couldn't stomach it. No matter how Parbati tried to hide it, Rajlakkhi Debi caught her out. "This—this is what you stole? You slut, how dare you!" Blinded by rage, the old, long-unused obscenity slid out of her mouth. Parbati began weeping helplessly. There would be no saving her today. She began pleading in desperate tones to try and extricate herself from this trouble, "Oh, *Didima*, you know that time when the votes were done and they kidnapped Niyoti and another girl from the *Nama Shudra* neighborhood, my mother ripped my father's *lungi* into rags and she wrapped me down there, under my pants before she hid me in the jute fields, oh, *Didima*. If the elections happen again, this time, *Didima*, I'll wear these before I hide . . . "

—translated from the Bengali by Shabnam Nadiya

KARA KAI WANG

Bird's Eye

On the phone with my mother last night
and it is the usual chatter—she's planted yellow
dahlias beneath the kitchen window and is trying
a new recipe with her bridge friends. Squirrels come up,
as they often do. My mother, for whom kindness
runs marrow in her bones, has a fierce, unwavering
dislike for squirrels. One I support but don't
understand. I find them sweet, digging holes
in her lawn, a garden party of acorns and burials.
On the gossip front she tells me M is unhappy
with her husband, but unwilling still to leave him,
how it makes her sad to see her friend so
tied down. The talk turns to my brother's new
in-laws, P and N, American, warm, and terribly
gracious. *We went on a hike yesterday,* my mother
tells me. Recounts how they saw a wild deer
eating from a tree, its two front legs suspended
in air. I think how years ago, I would have interjected,
All deer are wild, you don't have to say it. How unpleasant
and ordinary it would have been. Now bird's eye, I enter
and float and enter again. The gray strands in her voice
always catch me off guard. Our conversations I write down
without her knowing, without admitting why I do it.
She says N asked why she hasn't tried to meet anyone
after my father died. *You're so full of life and of interests,*
what man wouldn't want what you have to offer?
My mother, 65 and beautiful, tells me she's past the age
where she wants to offer someone something.
If it were your father it'd be a different story. She says this
as if the distance between them is a great stone church
and she is sitting in the last pew, light as perfume
along her neck. I watch her pat the empty seat beside her,

beckoning me to sit down. She holds my hand
as if she's asking for forgiveness, as if we are equals,
two grown women now, having lost the man we both loved.

BRUCE BOND

Book of Dolls 2

So tell me about your childhood,
the analyst asks the doll on the sofa.
And the doll looks back at him like,
Are you serious, and he looks back like,
No need to get defensive, and then, more
defensively, *Consider this a safe space.*
And you know now, it is not. I mean,
one minute you are no one, your head
full of cotton, and then, all the empty
chairs turn to you, the way a voice turns
toward an auditorium, and no one's there,
just a giant dark, and suddenly a doll
talks to you, somewhere in the emptiness,
in the silence that is your life as a child.

Book of Dolls 4

So tell me the first thing that comes to mind,
the doll says, holding up a blot of ink,
and I say, *I see ink inside the ink,*
and in that ink, a bed, inside the walls
a woman's voice weeping on the phone.
And he says, *Can you hear what she is*
saying. No, I say. *Try.* And I do.
Although I do not hear her clearly,
I hear the vague inflection of a *no,*
the note of some divorce or diagnosis,
I can't be sure, or, perhaps, remember.
There are no accidents, says the doll,
and although he is mistaken, I agree,
and on it goes, the voice inside a chaos
of ink, and the mother's answer, *no, no.*

Book of Dolls 7

The doll inside the doll inside the doll,
the last unbreakable doll at heart, says
one day when I'm unconscious, believe me,
I understand the feeling. I have been there.
Inside a sleep so deep it must be dreamless.
I have heard that doll in a mother's voice,
reading from a giant page with pictures.
The voice inside the voice and on and on.
It loves me still. Little wonder, as she
leaves, she leaves light burning in the hall.
I hear the child whose hall is always dark
and see things there no lamplight can reveal.
The dark thing inside the dark. I see it
still. The last dark that cannot be divided.

Book of Dolls 9

When I first pulled the string to make
her talk, she said what the doll-maker
thought I wanted to hear, that she loved
me, or rather, *you*, and *you*, whoever
you are, with the non-judgmental spirit
of a Jesus or machine. No small thing,
to think love might rise from the dead
to say without saying, *There is another*
world, and it is this one. But it got old.
And so, at last, I pulled the string out
like a needle in her back, and she said,
Yes, thank you, friend, as never before,
and then, more softly, *Dear God, thanks,*
as she slipped off into paradise, alone.

ADAM MEISNER

How to Pass through the Denkmal
für die ermordeten Juden Europas

If it's raining,
your umbrella will not fit through.
Take it down.
Get wet.

Now, proceed slowly—
there are too many intersections
for you to go quickly.
Climb the hills,
fall into the valleys,
stop to take a selfie.

No, don't take a selfie.

Okay, go ahead and take a selfie—
that German woman is taking one
(only try not to look sexy the way she's doing).

Start moving again.

Stop.
Feel sad.
Delete the selfie.

Think of what you'll do next.
Maybe a stop at Denkmal für die im Nationalsozialismus verfolgten Homosexuellen.
Or maybe more shopping.

Feel sad again.
Maybe it's the rain.
Maybe it's all the shopping.

Maybe you should go back to your hotel to dry off, watch BBC World News, and write about this.

Don't forget that you're still in the memorial.
Turn around and go back
to the exact place
where you entered.

Was it here?

Or here?

Or—

Promise yourself you will find meaning
in finding the exact place where you began.

1927–2017

For John Ashbery

For many years, obfuscation was
paramount. Which meant that each of us

had to hide out in his hermit kingdom.
Then light came one day in a dusty-rose

patina and all of us crept out as bluebells
dwarfed among the new grass.

Soon we learned to stand full height
and discovered that most of us were really giants.

Ergo it was decided that everybody needed his story
about how he first emerged as his smaller self

and then grew. My story was never any good—
no real beginning and certainly no climax. I had only

an ending: some terrible tragedy involving the pestilence.
Recently the storytelling has dwindled. We are

more lyrical than anything that can be told straight.
"Everyone back inside his wardrobe," someone orders.

I take up the command, but wonder if erasure might be
just as narcissistic as the transparency game.

It presumes, after all, that something of me might be missed.
Oh well. Here I go. Deep, deep into the mothballed furs.

JOHN GALLAHER

Sugarbomb

The new system at work is that we have donuts on Friday. I love
the new system. I think about Friday all week, and can easily toss
three donuts back, even if one's a glazed bowtie or a bear claw.
And then it's Birthday Party Day in the 4th Grade. This happens
approximately 15 times a year, with special days set aside in August
and January for those whose birthdays occurred over summer
and winter breaks. Bless, as they say, the beasts and children,
who also have a stake in how things turn out, even if they don't have
much of a say. Theirs are the pictures we most love to pass around,
kid dressed as a pumpkin, cat dressed as a banker. Hang in there,
baby, we say, and here's a cupcake for your trouble. It's been
a good year for baked goods. Because otherwise I only have
this rather ordinary life which spreads out across the room,
stopping at the TV, where all manner of things I'll never do
or experience happen, some travel shows or vacation house shows
in High Definition, which feel real enough that I can get pretty close
to fooling myself that I've been there. It's a form of intimacy,
how the final step of the falling-in-love game is to stare
into the other person's eyes for three minutes. I can see how
that might happen, so I'm never going to try it, except
with this donut. Think of it as a kind of burial at sea or baseball
game or lottery, really, use whatever metaphor you want, they all
kind of work the same, how I'm amused by the idea that much
of the culture of the 20th Century was built on plastics, how
we thought plastic was going to last forever, and so we would too,
and it's already, fifty years later, degrading. Oh 20th Century
empire-building irony. On the other hand, Oh no! All that stuff!
And some of it was great! The future's rough, and so is
the candidate they have looking back at us, holding out a cupcake,
saying "I'd never forget your birthday." Something like that
was in the movie *Brazil*, a place I'm sure I've been to, all
bright yellow houses full of the smell of coffee and rainforest.

ANDREA COHEN

Circular

Everyone with two
hands has options.
He stuck one
in the circular
saw he was being
taught to run.
It was his first
day at the factory.
He knew what
they were making:
a man he didn't
mean to be.
After it happened,
he held both arms
up—like a prize-
fighter might. There
was blood every-
where, and bits
of bone, there
was a whole
life before him,
and someone packing
that hand in ice, in
case some son-
of-a-bitch might
try to reattach
him to the circle
he was leaving.

Eavesdropping on Adam and Eve

It didn't get interesting
until after they'd left.
An extended vacation,
Adam called it. *R&*
D, Eve said. *Whatever.*
In Eden, they never
said so much as
pass the salt on
account of everything
tasting so great there.
They were strangers
until they left, when
Adam confessed, *I*
felt penned in there,
and Eve, forgetting how
naked they'd been,
said, *I was always*
waiting for the other
shoe to drop. Now
they're both cobblers, now
they have so much
to talk about: whether
to spring for heat
or vaccines, whether
to call their interiors
climate or weather,
when the next ice age
might hit. Adam pours
himself another
hieroglyph and asks:
what does it all mean?
and Eve does what
she always does:
wraps herself, boa-
like, around him and holds
the camera an arm's

length above for a
this is us moment
for the snake they
miss so much.

Civil War

I had one son
who always played

capture the flag
in the dark—

and another son
who played another

game with him—
capturing the dark

in a flag.

PATRICK KINDIG

the carmelites: a chorus

after francis poulenc

when the revolution came
        the nuns thought it best
                to die. they donned their habits

& clutched their rosaries & went out
        into the world to do it. by
                the end of the day, the bodies of nuns

were everywhere: dead nuns
        hanging from the sycamore
                trees, dead nuns lining

the gorge. they piled themselves
        into subway cars, onto highways,
                threw their trembling bodies from

the tops of lighthouses. soon
        the revolution ground to
                a halt, its bright & bloody gears

clogged with torn habits. when
        the leaders left their bunkers
                to survey what was left

of the world, they found it littered
        with an impossible number
                of nuns. the sun rose

as it always did. the breeze
        picked up. & throughout the earth
                there was a tremendous

rustling, countless
    white veils whispering
        now & at the hour of our death—

BILL MARSH

Free Forever

IN THE WEEKS AFTER HE DIED, up to and including the morning we scattered his ashes at the base of a crumbling oak tree, no one used the word *suicide* to describe my older brother's final act. To me it seemed obvious. There'd been a clear pattern—reckless binges ending in detox, treatment programs, phoned-in assurances disintegrating into more binges, more detox. From a distance it looked deliberate if not premeditated, willful if noncommittal. "We knew this was coming," my sister said in the woods that day, but by then "this" had morphed into just that, an empty cipher, a pronoun wrested from its fatal antecedent.

It had rained the night before. When the wind blew, raindrops slipped from the branches overhead into our folded hands, pelted the leafy carpet at our feet. We stood in a circle using words to make sense of things. The instructions had been clear: personal reflections and stories, purely voluntary, no pressure to speak. For weeks I'd been planning on silence, a stony refusal to play along, but when my turn came I caved, uttered a few half-baked phrases about good times and bad, my older brother's penchant for arbitrary generosity, often despite himself. It was a lousy performance, a low pass at best. I was the weakest link, by far, in an otherwise heartfelt group mourning activity.

It's possible I had misunderstood the assignment, the *prompt* that comes with the death of a loved one. When my sister called with the news, I was standing at a window watching two squirrels play a precarious game of tag in the leafy treetops. Seconds later I was doubled over in a chair, quietly weeping—step one in a grieving process the experts say may last a lifetime. But then old habits kicked in. I'm a professor who assigns a lot of essays, so before long I'd constructed a provisional thesis (slow suicide) and sought evidence in a muddle of memories, thoughts, feelings. Psychologists say this kind of "grief work" is normal, an act of cognitive restructuring which, in my case, was blatantly "past-based" in its focus on my older brother's self-destructive actions. By contrast my mother, who at 78 had to reckon with the sudden death of her middle-aged son, found solace in Catholicism, the afterlife, and a future untroubled by prolonged personal suffering. My younger sister turned to herbal infusions and the chakras, my father to thin fragments of memory poking through his dementia, and so on.

All perfectly normal, once again. But it's precisely the *normal* I want to explore here, for starters. Grief assumes different forms depending on the nature of the death, the predilections of the bereaved, and one's structuring orientation (as individual, as social being) to the stories we tell in the interest of closure, in our collective efforts to make sense and move on. Confronted with loss, one's first impulse is to step back and take a closer look, to analyze and interpret, to revise understandings—of the world, ourselves, belief systems, each other. Death comes with open questions and no easy answers. Death prods and provokes, propels research and inquiry. Like most assignments, death presents a most difficult learning challenge.

INVENTION

Grieving is inherently collaborative, and it turns out I don't do group work very well. As the third of five children I never fretted my role as the middle child, so when my brother died, in the midst of my sadness and self-recriminations (*could* I have done more?), I assumed I could ride out this latest family crisis as I had in the past, buffered on both sides, cradled *in the middle* of the agonizing action. In small groups there are always the load-bearers, the leaders who step forward and take charge; and there are followers happy to abide, let the process unfold. I was content to follow, knowing full well that my place in the lineup—my differentiated role in this group formation—had little bearing on how much (or little) actual work I would do moving forward.

Initial phone calls were cathartic, mutually supportive, but then hard decisions had to be made, consensus reached. Certain skills seemed appropriate to the task—critical thinking, organization, note-taking—but in the early going I lacked the nerve to front these skills in any productive way. My older brother had lived something of a loner's life far removed from the rest of us in a two-story house north of Reno. He had no partner, no kids. His dog, a boxer mix named Bella, had run away years ago. A hospital admin emailed a helpful "next steps" brochure listing local mortuaries and options for my brother's remains. But what about the house? Was it secure? Maybe we could ask a neighbor to walk over and check. What were my brother's final wishes? Burial? Cremation? In Nevada? Back home in Illinois? None of us knew offhand, but one of us could fly out, wade through his papers, look for a will—assuming he'd left one. One of us should make the trip, but who?

I fell mute at this point in the conversation, both wanting to participate and refusing to do so. The task seemed overwhelming, the timing awful. Who could commit on such short notice? My resistance was counterproductive, childish even, but what a relief when my younger brother—a team manager in the corporate world, a load-bearer—broke the silence and volunteered to go. I felt instantly guilty, like I'd botched it, missed a chance to step up. My guilt deepened when I realized what I wanted most was to avoid responsibility, to slide into the cozy middle, committed to the overall project but averse to any actual fieldwork. Faced with a problem none of us had asked for, my first impulse was to oppose, to contest what felt, deep down, like an imposition, an assault, a torquing of my attention.

Again, all normal. Death pulls us out of one framework (a comfort zone) and drops us into another. We the bereaved are framed—by convention, protocol, discursive practices—as much as we work to frame ourselves and each other in a context forever changed by death. Emotional fallout can be extreme, but in the weeks after my brother died my emotions ranged from low-grade sadness to an easy surrender, a pat reconciliation with the predictable and foregone (*we knew this was coming*). If there are phases to grief, mine progressed so quickly I had to wonder if there was something wrong with me. Later, after research, I understood such moments of self-censure make sense in a society that polices bereavement, that teaches us to measure our own reactions against cultural norms and behavioral codes. When someone dies, it seems we should know from the outset how to think and feel, then how to navigate, interpolate, and assess our thoughts and feelings. If we don't know, we can always look to the more experienced, the favored archetypes of this age-old practice. Models are everywhere: among family and friends, on TV, in books and movies. Meanwhile, those who for whatever reason don't conform—who grieve too much, at the wrong time, or not at all—are labeled *aberrant* in the face of normal grief work. I was somewhat relieved, in fact, to learn that the "wrong" in me was perfectly *all right* from this broader theoretical perspective. As aberration, I had a social role to play. I belonged insofar as I was an emotional outsider, a raging doubter, a grief iconoclast, a weak link in the bereavement chain.

I also bristled at some obvious contradictions as my family began the tough work of remembering my brother. We were planning his memorial—a long, recursive process of compiling, sorting, ranking, framing, and publishing the details of his life. To be honest I found this phase of the assignment fascinating, in part because I learned so much about my brother after he died. Our task was to brainstorm facts, images, stories. There were questions about emphasis—what to highlight, what to ignore. "Can you please send me the three words you would use to describe him?" my younger sister prompted in an early email. She had volunteered to create a memorial website and needed help with what the grief scholars call the "back story" of my brother's life, as opposed to the "event story," the circumstances surrounding his death, which no one cared to discuss. She'd attached two photos, wanted to know which would serve better on the website main page. One showed a cleanly shaved white man in a dark gray suit and lavender tie, hair tightly cropped, bright blue eyes over a pearly smile. The other captured my brother as a scruffy outdoorsman: dark sunglasses, shirtless and deeply tanned, fishing pole in one hand, prize catch in the other. Both accurate, equally celebratory for different reasons. So how do we choose?

This part of grief work is all about relationships, specifically the "realignment" of personal relationships via narrative reconstruction. The stories we tell may be "subject to dynamic reconstruction over time," as Robert Neimeyer and co-authors write in the journal *Death Studies*, but in the memorial moment, when the shock of loss rubs up against the need to make sense of it, what matters most is the speedy construction of a comprehensive, preferably favorable plot line. It's a daunting task, to narrate a loved one's life in a compressed, consumable format. I found the challenge overwhelming, but in response to my sister's request for three words my mother sent four that stuck: *Spiritual, Honorable, Charitable, Lovable.* There were follow-up questions about old friends and girlfriends, about my brother's early career as a computer programmer at Texas Instruments and later as a systems engineer for a private Defense Department contractor in San Diego. My younger brother, now on site in Reno, found a résumé he could scan and send to my sister, who had opted for a "free forever online" memorial service offering an "everlasting presence" for the deceased and "a virtual interactive family tree for future generations to come." Expectations were high, to say the least. We all agreed my dead brother's clean-cut professional look would serve best for front-page optics.

DEVELOPMENT

Some stories never made it onto the free-forever website. My first drunk at the age of twelve, for example, came with the help of my fifteen-year-old brother. It was an eye-opening night, followed by a morning I wish I could forget. I'm not judging or casting blame here. To the contrary, there were clear advantages to having an older sibling with a magician's knack for scoring booze. He had friends who could buy it, friends with older brothers and sisters who could buy it. All impediments vanished when he himself reached the legal drinking age. With his aid and approval I traded paychecks from my afterschool job for a steady supply of Stroh's twelve-packs, which I kept hidden in my bedroom closet behind crates stuffed with sci fi novels. We had that in common, too—a passion for Heinlein, Le Guin, Clarke, Asimov, with me always one book behind in the trilogies.

At sixteen I spent a weekend with my older brother at college. He'd joined a fraternity famous for its Friday keggers. The pubs down on University Avenue carded at the door, but I got in no problem using his expired student ID. I stayed drunk for two days straight, finally crashed in a blown-out bean bag chair while down below raged what the frat boys referred to as an "all-nighter on the quad." Two years later I started my freshman year at the same university. I'd just finished decorating the walls of my dorm room when my older brother, now a fifth-year senior, showed up with a fifth of Jack Daniels—"to share with your new friends," he said. By night's end, with Jack's help, I'd made quite a few.

It's so easy now, with the benefit of hindsight and database research, to see the pattern, one common to many families, especially those with the means and where-withal to scaffold experiences of this order. Psychologists who study substance abuse and sibling relationships note that an older sibling's excesses can lead to increased risk factors for the younger. It's an obvious case of behavioral modeling, rendered even riskier when the sibling relationship is marked by conflict and coercive interactions, as ours was from day one. Usually the fights with my brother weren't too extreme, but some, during our teen years especially, involved fists and kitchen knives (wielded but never used) and the occasional chair hurled across the room. When I read in one journal that a sibling relationship grounded in conflict can lead to antisocial behaviors later in life, I had to stop and wonder. Our fights didn't end but rather *evolved* as we got older. Once as young adults we were camping with friends in the High Sierra. The fire had died down and all the ice in the cooler had melted when something—a poor-ly placed word, I guess—sparked an antisocial interaction that one friend described afterward as "two brothers going at it." I woke up the next day with a sore wrist and a bruised ego. I was still furious, but mostly I felt hurt and embarrassed, convinced my brother and I simply didn't get along and never would. He surprised me by choosing to bury the incident in a fog of post-drunk blackout. "Did we have a fight last night?" he asked squeamishly, pleading ignorance. And that was the end of it.

According to the grief experts, these stories we choose to remember—the ones that go public, the ones we keep to ourselves—are just small 'n' narratives in a much larger process of *narrating grief*. As one would expect, the process is really more about *us* than the deceased. Behind the impulse to order information and construct back story is a deeper need to reaffirm, repair, or replace the defining plot and theme of our own life stories. We do this retrospective work at every level, seeking stability and security, as Neimeyer et al. write, in both "simple habit structures" and "personal and collective cosmologies" destabilized by loss. One day in the midst of our memorial planning my younger brother confessed by email that he was "only remembering the good times" (my dead brother's *generosity* and *helpfulness*, in particular) and "having a hard time" remembering the bad. To be sure, none of us harbored any illusions about my brother's addiction. We'd all witnessed the destruction (to body and property) firsthand. We'd lost patience, too, with his myopic refusal to accept help, our offers often met with derision and an empty, narcissistic claim that he could manage his recovery just fine on his own. And yet my little brother found stability and security in a cosmology of grace and forgiveness, in reaffirming goodness. I guess most people would do the same under similar circumstances. "I suppose it's human nature," he proposed.

But I still had my doubts, was still fixated, for better or worse, on the bad and difficult. I thought about this a lot as the assignment progressed from the *planning* to the *drafting* stage. Group work was going well, by all appearances. We'd identified a place to scatter my brother's ashes: a grand oak grove on the family farm, where as kids we'd spent our summers fishing the river and paddling canoes. I'd volunteered to handle the catering arrangements, and since I now made my home on the farm I was the one who signed off when the ashes arrived via UPS. The box felt a lot heavier than I'd expected, and I'd given no thought to short-term storage. Quite possibly it was "human nature" that guided me downstairs to the basement, where I placed my brother's boxed remains on a low shelf, wedged between a Coleman cooler and some old camping gear. I swear this wasn't intentional, but I admit it felt right in the moment. Because that's how I remember my brother, through good times and bad: by himself in a low dark place, roughing it out in nature, equipment ready to hand.

Feedback

When the website launched, tributes and condolences started rolling in. My younger sister set the tone with a brief note addressed to her dead brother: "You are now where you have always yearned to be," she wrote. "You are with God. You are free. You are whole. You are ascended." This would be a common theme—my brother's freedom and wholeness in death, his ascension to a better place, one "full of delight," as one friend later added. Another friend took it a step further and booked my brother a seat on the Starship Enterprise. "These are the voyages . . . His continuing mission . . ."—and so on. One couple, reaffirming their belief in "God's word the Bible," quoted Acts 24:15, which (I'll assume this is accurate) speaks to the "resurrection of both the righteous and the unrighteous." One contributor lauded my brother's "bright spirit," while others, finding solace in the secular, celebrated his intelligence, quick wit, "manliness," and cooking skills. One old girlfriend wrote glowingly of my brother's talents as a handyman, his ability to "fix anything" (boat, Jeep, toilet). He liked to sing, too—ABBA, early Genesis, old TV theme songs—sometimes at odd times and without warning. Sometimes he whistled so loud it "hurt my ears."

Except for the Bible bits, this all sounded familiar. While no Trekkie, my brother could recite entire scenes from the original Star Trek series, having cycled through all seventy-odd episodes at least half a dozen times. And true, his pop music repertoire had peaked circa 1986, but he had good pipes and a top-notch stereo system, as his neighbors back in San Diego would attest. Nor would I ever deny my brother his handyman skills, which came easily and served all of us well. There's plenty more, but by the time I swallowed my pride and took a dive into the memorial website, I'd already formed an opinion—of the whole exercise, not just the clunky free-forever tribute page. What an ugly mess, this death business. What a travesty, our collective search for "new meaning" in the ruins of a troubled life. I'd had it with the hedging and sidestepping, the half truths and obfuscation, the artificial "realignments" via storylines that to me seemed miles off the mark, no closer to resurrection than Captain Kirk's receding hairline. From my vantage as a critical thinker—one who'd opted, admittedly, to sit back and watch the process unfold—I couldn't stomach the assignment anymore, our joint effort to reinvent my brother in the interest of "remembering the good." It felt like a cover-up, a sham, a lie, a whitewash.

It so happens I was reading George Yancy at the time, whose unflinching analysis of white primacy in the United States felt like a rebuke directed straight at me and my family's grief work. Nothing but a thin film of screen residue separated the "ascension" rhetoric flaring up on the memorial website from Yancy's definition of whiteness as "the transcendental norm" by which self-identified white people "live their lives as persons, individuals." It was all too easy, actually, the manner in which my brother in death, my family in life—in our words and deeds, our robust planning, our selective storytelling—latched onto the whiteness "norm" and gave it concrete form and substance. But there it was, in plain text on the free-forever website: the historical meta-narrative informing these mawkish tributes, each one an attempt to reaffirm my brother's atomic individuality, his innocence, his manliness and "exclusive transcendence." The more I read, the more I found myself trapped under the bright light of this heady text-to-self connection. I felt my own sense of off-world levity, a kind of *liftoff* into regions unknown. And yet it all seemed so banal, so familiar and ultimately disappointing, as when a mask comes off to reveal the same mask underneath.

There are few checks on transcendence, evidently, when it comes to white people. As Yancy notes, we tend to see ourselves, "even if unconsciously," as "abstract minds," as "spectral beings" always already balanced on the edge of preeminence. My older brother had kept a tidy house, but when he died he left a gory mess: blood and feces smeared on walls, tamped into carpets, a dozen or so Skyy vodka bottles scattered about, dead soldiers one and all. My younger brother called from Reno to share the details and commiserate, having spared my aging parents and two sisters. "They don't need to know this," he said. But several weeks later, standing in the woods, he spoke metaphorically of his older brother's "messiness" as a human being, his on-off moods, his blowups, his knee-jerk fighting words. These traits did not signal "malice," my brother insisted, because he never really meant the things he said. "It was just the way he was, it was in his DNA." He was innocent, in short, because his actions weren't grounded in intention. When my mother spoke, she focused on her son's roller-coaster successes and failures. He'd made a lot of money writing code in the late nineties, then lost it all in the early 2000s trying to outsmart Wall Street from the privacy of his ergonomic home office. But this carelessness, too, was in character, hardcoded into his DNA. He'd always been a special child, *hyperactive* before the word became popular. Extra innocent, in other words.

"Suffering from an excess of positive attributes," my wife later summarized, to which I added another bit from Yancy about the "privileges and immunities" enjoyed by us white people, white men especially, for whom "the world opens up" as a space of achievement and "expansive motility." My brother was looking for work when he died, his fortune dried up, his house newly mortgaged. From my mother's perspective, though, his bumpy ride through life was still "expansive" if in reverse, his drive and ambition vectoring back to a nascent pureness and potential, his substance abuse the dark interior of an otherwise uncomplicated transubstantiation. When she placed a small crucifix on the box containing my brother's ashes, I read the gesture as an act of desperation, a grieving mother's last-ditch effort to renegotiate (the only way she knew how) her prodigal son's dubious relationship with a God he never knew.

REVISION

For our family gathering we'd settled on a basic program: (1) personal thoughts and feelings followed by (2) the scattering of ashes and then (3) individual or group prayers, at one's discretion. We'd all agreed to conduct ourselves *as my brother would have wanted*, so the three-part structure seemed appropriate given his fluctuating attention, in life, to things spiritual. Some Reno friend insisted my older brother had "accepted Jesus Christ" in the end, but with the exception of my mother we were skeptical. He may have dabbled in Christianity, during his AA days especially, but like me he'd exited the church as a teenager and never looked back. As an adult he practiced sitting meditation during a lengthy pop Zen phase, loaned me a copy of *The Power of Now*. But there was also that time when he spoke openly of his belief in conspiratorial overlords hovering off-planet, installing politicians and dictating policy while micromanaging his every thought and action. In light of this, the family had decided to officiate communally rather than call in a priest or pastor. My mother condoned the decision, but I could tell she wasn't pleased. "Will someone remind me of the limitations other than prayer?" she emailed later, her deep suspicion of religious intolerance only thinly veiled as a procedural question. No one responded, but my diplomatic younger brother offered to call her and clear the air.

Meanwhile, as the day neared, I had to turn my attention to more earthly matters. The ten-day forecast predicted rain and heavy winds. The ceremonial grove would be soggy, the rain potentially prohibitive. And those ancient oak trees sloughing dead branches—what if one were to snap off mid-service, bonk someone on the head? I found real comfort in these and other concrete concerns. I was also deep into grief theory now, asking questions that yielded no easy answers, so as a kind of survival tactic I decided to proceed in the guise of an ethnographer, a participant-observer. What better way to ride out this ugly storm than to place another frame around my family's grief framework and *take lots of notes*? I opened a new file on my computer, created a dedicated iCloud note on my phone. And when, just days before the memorial, my kid sister surprised us with a last-minute program change, I took a deep breath and stayed calm, let the moment unfold as if I were just living it.

"I'd like to do 2 things for our private family ceremony if no one objects," my sister wrote by email. I didn't know this yet, but her proposed amendments (play a song, read a poem) made perfect sense given the sense-making urgency of this or any mourning activity. When someone dies, we struggle to find meaning for the sake of our own fragile life stories. We do this to lift ourselves out of grief, to navigate the pain, to stabilize a self-narrative thrown off-balance by loss. Given the seriousness and difficulty of the task, it can help sometimes to scaffold the effort, seeking support in "discursive resources" ready to hand, like songs, prayers, and poems. My older sister liked the idea. My younger brother and I balked. A de facto gender divide opened up that may or may not have meant something.

For my own part I resented the request because it felt like yet another imposition, a form of memory colonization. My younger sister (I believed) wanted to stamp preferred meaning, via her favorite song, onto my dead brother's choppy, multilayered life. In response I urged caution, championed the "simplicity and openness" of the original plan. In truth what turned me off were the *words*. I'd found the song online then sat back and quietly fumed, ethnographer's cap tossed decisively to the corner. The selection itself ("Love is Still the Answer" by Jason Mraz) is irrelevant. Important to me was the storyline, what the grief psychologists might call the "dominant narrative" embedded in the lyrics. Scaffolding is one thing (I muttered in the background), rogue efforts to regulate the "proper performance" of grief another. Such narratives are like thick fog on a wet gloomy morning—sticky, dangerously impenetrable, obfuscating. They surround and entrap, disabling the performances of those (like me) who would rather perform differently. Sometimes the stories correspond, but just as often they clash with the personal predilections of the bereaved. The mere thought of that song playing in the woods set my teeth on edge. I felt totally *clashed with*, subjugated, trapped once again in a false and falsifying narrative headspace.

But was I being fair? The answer depends, of course, on whom you ask. As a student of life I understood what most of us do, even without further research—that the stories we choose to tell about our dead loved ones (and ourselves) are necessarily reductive, sugar-coated. They show us the good side at a safe remove: sun-dappled forest, not the snarling gremlins crouching in the trees. So why my precious insistence on *simplicity*? Why my fear of *regulation* and *subjugation*? After all, I'd already promised myself a conspicuous silence at the scattering. Who cares what words saturated the creeping fog around me? What's more, as a professor committed to notions of process and recursivity, why did I rise up in opposition to this eleventh-hour change? My students get rewarded, praised for such moments of bold last-minute revision.

My sister got a cold let-down, a definitive *thanks but no thanks.* "I just thought you all would like the song," she wrote in the end, deflated.

But then there was also the matter of the poem, the second half of my sister's two-part proposal. My older brother had authored it (a brief lyric entitled "I Am") during his mindfulness phase, and I fully admit now the text has bearing as both a tender nod to self-narrative reconstruction and a compelling take on Yancy's "transcendental norm," not to mention the memorial website's prevailing ascension motif. As it turns out, my sister did read the poem but toward the end, during the program's voluntary prayer segment, just after we'd scattered my brother's ashes at the base of a moribund oak tree. I didn't hear the whole text, had wandered off into the dripping woods to gather acorns and commune with my preferred predilections. I wandered back just in time, though, to catch the final line: "I am me, I am here, I am now." A big tree shielded the action as I pulled out my phone and transcribed.

REFLECTION

Essays have always pretended to be honest reflections, "drawn from life" without striving or artifice, as Michel de Montaigne wrote in the opening appeal of his *Essais.* "Here I want to be seen in my simple, natural everyday fashion," the author penned with a hearty rhetorical wink, "for it is my own self that I am painting." Much has been written about this contrivance, about the essayist's seductive framing of a 'simple' self for the benefit of a reader tasked, on the receiving end, with the artifice of playing along. To read a personal essay at face value is to reach an agreement with the author: yes, I am willing to see what you *want to be seen.* The payoff can be awesome, for here, as Montaigne writes, "you will read of my defects and my native form" but only as "social convention allows." This threshold—the limitations imposed by social convention—is a hard line in the sand of personal confession, integral to narrative performance. The essay may only fictionalize, as Bruce Ballenger writes, our "fascination with the self in motion," but without that fiction, without social conventions limiting the fiction, there would be no motion, no self, no fascination.

The same appears to be true of human grief work. When my brother died, his death (event and back story) brought on a moment of cognitive upheaval. But it's not only death that does this. Any loss or really any major life disturbance can *heave up* and put the skids on our everyday habits, grounding assumptions, and structuring orientations. To restore balance and purpose, we get busy learning our way back to security and stability, leveraging old and new "habits of mind" and invoking, where necessary, a "spirit of inquiry" to answer life's tough questions. We gather together and tell stories. We share resources. We revisit and sometimes restructure beliefs. We reexamine and often reaffirm controlling themes in our own lives. We *narrate our grief* in order to see and be seen by those around us.

We also police our own and other's grief work. Sometimes "society" does the policing for us, instructing the bereaved how to think and feel, labeling as "aberrant" those who do not comply. For many of us, racist metanarratives underwrite our scriptural interventions, and while we may live in a society that pretends to be postracist, it's hard to ignore the fundamental racism of one theme in particular. For white people, it may be "human nature" to bracket personal defects in the interest of narrative wholeness and perfection. (I want to portray myself "whole" and "wholly naked," Montaigne wrote.) It may be "normal" to seek transcendence in a world always opening up before us, where even in death we expand and occupy, always *me*, always *here*, always *now*. But analysis shows that a tragic story reverse-engineered to guarantee a happy ending is just that—a story turned inside out and told in reverse, a restoration project in service to a false ideal.

Without question I too participate, even as I stand back, phone in hand, to observe and record. I take stock of my core assumptions, seeking meaning in a cognitive restructuring activity that may do little more, in the end, than reaffirm the transcendental norm I seek to dismantle. Taking refuge in critique and correction, I take out my pen and paint "aberrant grief" in the margins of this confession. I find comfort in the contrivance because I can operate both within and against the central action with its false appearances and annoying obfuscations. In framing the action from what feels like an outside, I make way nonetheless for process and healing, for cognitive restructuring and realignment, on the inside. I show myself in my native form—because all that early resentment and failure is real stuff, real fallout. Anything so painful and difficult must be real, right? Or is my pain, or rather the strange relief I feel in the absence of pain, also a contrivance, a simple fascination with my (white) self in motion?

In the end, a story takes shape. The story, developed at a distance, serves as a culmination, a grief-work capstone, an exercise in metacognitive exorcism. To pull it off I have to believe, or at least pretend to believe, in the essay as a truth-telling organism. I know full well that essays are nothing of the kind, that they are fictions masquerading as unmediated revelations. Still I insist—by force of habit and western literary tradition—that any action playing out on stage is *true*. My brother's death, our multiple responses, the trope of ascension, the myth of white transcendence, the pains and pleasures of rhetorical honesty—this, all of it, is what I want to be seen.

But what about the *unseen*, the truths we can't or won't tell? I'm several drafts into this essay when I remember something important—a game my older brother used to play, a crude abandonment game the neighborhood cool kids called "ditching." The rules were simple (ditch the little one), the results hard to measure since the literal object of the game (the one ditched) was left behind to wallow in an unexpected solitude. Back then, choking on the dust of those frequent ditchings, I felt both targeted and implicated, singled out and unfairly played. I also understood, even then, that my brother's sudden departure, while cruel, was meant to teach me a lesson, namely that my inherent ditchability implied that I, too, could play the ditcher one day, with my own younger brother perhaps. I never liked the game, never saw the point really, let alone the fun in it, which may explain why this little bit of back story didn't surface until late in the process. The symbolism, of course, is glaring, embarrassing almost: when he died, my brother ditched me for good, leaving me stranded and "wholly naked," attentive to little more than the awful distance between us. Should I assume, in choosing to add the story here, that I'm back where I started, losing the game all over again?

Translation Folio

TOMASZ RÓŻYCKI

Translator's Introduction

Mira Rosenthal

Composed in the pivotal years leading up to its 2016 publication—with populism on the rise across eastern Europe and authoritarianism growing in Poland—Tomasz Różycki's *Letter by Letter* takes a hard yet existential look at the state of human affairs in the 21st century. "If I had to sum up the last few years in a single sentence," Różycki said recently in an interview, "the phrase 'I wish you were here' captures it best. This expression is just as relevant if we say it to a god, to someone who is absent or deceased, or to the other half of one's own 'I.'" Taking this phrase as its basis for repetitions and riffs, the collection builds a dialog of longing for an absent hero—by turns angelic messenger, police detective, beloved, and, in a sense, the poet himself—who might be able to rescue 21st-century human beings from a sense of emptiness and despair.

Themes of displacement, belonging, and a divided sensibility have always been central to Różycki's poetry as an aspect of what I would call a historical consciousness. His poems combine highly specific imagery with evocative references to the history of his family and his region. He has lived his whole life in Opole, a previously German city that was repopulated by Poles forcibly relocated from Lwów (in what is now Ukraine) when borders shifted West after WWII. His poems situate this layering of identities and histories within a very personal, at times hermetic world—often literally within the human body itself—reminding us again of mortality but also of what he calls elsewhere our "beautiful and miraculous singularity."

Such themes resonate in *Letter by Letter* through a stunning balancing act between political inflection and existential questioning. For example, the poem "Anger in the Bank" (included here) proposes a hypothetical world in which there is "justice at last in how to allocate our pain" and a full accounting of past political actions—profiteering, sabotage, perversion—that have undermined true representative government. However, this democratic peace quickly breaks down into the usual repetitions of despicable behavior, and we are left in a world where freedom has been reduced to a choice between the electric collar or isolation, to a world in which a vast sea subsumes the individual's voice.

But the speaker's recognition of pattern—also invoked through the use of a recurring form—leads not to despair but to an affirmation of the importance of love and individual connection. I see an avowal of love in a number of the poems in this selection—even if love is a dog, perhaps rabid, who has escaped into the open after tearing the house to shreds. Or, a recognition of love comes in a dream of someone deceased and passed over to the other side. "I woke as if I'd just been fished from the stream," the speaker admits, coming back to this world with an intense longing to touch the body of the beloved again. These poems capture the oneiric quality that critics have recognized in much of Różykci's work. They combine memory of the dead and what does not yet exist, merging the dreamlike qualities of past and future in an endless moment of hesitation in the present.

Time and again throughout *Letter by Letter*'s cycle of 99 poems, the speaker longs for love as a redemptive power in the present; writing, on the other hand, remains suspect. As Anna Spólna has pointed out, for Różycki, the figure of the poet as priest and poetry as sacred turns out to be as unbearable as the image of an artist as clown and the poem as a transgressive step into the profane. I see this acute awareness in "Second Poem for Menelik," in which letters, the very building blocks of words, become a means by which some higher power (God? Death?) carries out a "master plan to build a great black hole" that will reduce all of us and everything to nothing one day. Writing, then, is a stay against this ultimate loss and a desire for intimacy—the direct address of "I wish you were here." At the same time, it is an act that confirms the speaker's loneliness and a recognition of how words fail to bring us close. Instead, the speaker encloses in an envelope a single sprig of mint, a singular sign of life that carries a belief in beauty, even as we pass into that great black hole.

The direct address to the African emperor Menelik, which happens a number of times throughout the collection, allows Różycki to explore an interesting intertwining of political and poetic history. Drawing on his background in French literature, Różykci nods to Arthur Rimbaud's role in African military efforts in the nineteenth century. After denouncing poetry, the enfant terrible of the Parisian literary scene of the 1870s settled in the Ethiopian city of Harar, where he made a living by trading in coffee and firearms. Rimbaud famously provided weapons to Menelik, which likely helped the emperor defeat Italy when the country invaded Ethiopia in 1896. The speaker of Różycki's collection writes to Menelik as a way to resist joining him—perhaps in political power, perhaps in death, perhaps in the profiteering way Menelik took advantage of Rimbaud by duping him out of what was fully owed to him.

The most challenging aspect of presenting individual poems from *Letter by Letter* is exactly the fact of this kind of thematic circling back. The more you read, the more you hear the poems talking to each other, layering history, increasing connection. And this I find perfectly fitting for a collection built on the direct address. Różycki thinks of each of his collections as a composed whole; he writes a book, not individual poems. The poems never exist for him separate from the effect of all of them in conversation, just as we each never exist separate from the history that informs our present and already has designs on our future. I hope this selection entices you into the colloquy of the whole collection—once I finish translating it!

TOMASZ RÓŻYCKI : Five Poems

Anger in the Bank

Let's say you've won—some future revolution
and redistribution of goods, with all the oppressed
eagerly writing laws. Representative government.
Justice at last in how to allocate our pain,

the presidential couple promising good news.
Lieutenant Anielewicz tracks down all perverts,
saboteurs, profiteers. It takes some years.
Then someone streetside chucks a stone again.

At night again in the market square a crowd,
irate, manipulated, serving evil still?
When enemies are near, all education
goes down the drain, there's merely engineering,

routine injections and reports. Electric collars,
or isolation, going somewhere far away,
where there's a black and white expanse, a flapping sky,
and just beyond the bars a sea that drinks the voice.

In Two Days

Two days, and it will be the sixteenth winter.
I dreamed you walked upstairs yourself and said
that everything is fine now with your leg,
a new doctor. He has me in a state-

of-the-art hospital. You looked much younger,
and really happy. Though I knew that it
must be a lie, I laughed, I laughed and somehow
like an idiot turned my head away

so that you wouldn't see. Of course, you had
a present for each of the children, and of course
I couldn't touch you—standing by the exit
since you had to get back. I woke as if

I'd just been fished from the stream. Winter sunlight
cuts through the eyelid like a scalpel, hangs the eye
with an earring made of ice that will melt
in two days, five, a week, a month from now.

Cracks

And if you do exist—just say—are you
inside of me somewhere? Growing like fungus,
a lump, a foreign body, stardust, cosmic cancer,
from day to day, from year to year, infesting

my territory, seizing land, inciting a coup
one certain dawn in winter. Then you'll rule
with absolute power inside my body thanks to
advancements in conversion surgery to turn into

your likeness, which means nothing, right? If you are there
you are an enemy within, your own antithesis,
an agent, saboteur, and every night you feed
on me, bite by bite, right? It's no coincidence

that every morning in the glass I see more traces
of pretense creeping in and diagnose my face
as having someone else's cracks, lines, wrinkles,
a foreign sentence added, not in my own hand.

Open

Judging by the signs of struggle, busted
furniture, traces of blood, these small bite marks,
it must have been love, Lieutenant. The trail
leads past the gas station to the empty tract

behind the factory. I'd recognize love anywhere,
if only by its smell. Last summer I drove it
out to the ocean, and the whole car reeked.
And even now I sense it. All the way back

it kept moaning and whining there in the seat,
until I let it out at night. Forty-five stitches
and scars, but still standing. And I won't make
the same mistake twice. I'm packing some heat

and a box of extra bullets in my sleeve.
It can survive on dust but can't hold out
for long alone and in the end must come to us.
I'll leave the kitchen light on and the door ajar.

Second Poem for Menelik

I'll not be coming after all, letters are crawling
all over me, swarming like earwigs, leeches.
Forgive me, but this rash is itchy, scratching useless.
And training doesn't help, standing in formation,

infantry songs—I sort them into ranks
of foreign-sounding quotes and watch them fight—
they bite each other some but bite me more.
They die faster than sunlight, but this allergy

returns with increased strength at night, so I
collect them one by one and shackle them
like galley slaves, stanza by stanza, hundred
by hundred on a paper ship. They'll come in handy,

I've heard you use them in your master plan
to build a great black hole. Inside this envelope
I send no period, just a sprig of mint plucked yesterday,
a sign this world remains shockingly beautiful.

—translated from the Polish by Mira Rosenthal

VINCENT CZYZ

Enchantments

At dawn on September 16, 1810, in the Mexican Village of Dolores, Padre Miguel Hidalgo uttered his cry for freedom from Spanish rule. The famous call to rebellion has since become known as El Grito de Dolores.

HERE, EDUARDO WILL TELL YOU, is the magic: When he wasn't looking, two weeks were turned into 12 years. *Abracadabra.* He will hold out his black bowler (a magnificently round fit atop his bald head) to show it is as empty and echoing as the plundered tomb of a Mayan king. Then he will laugh.

Twelve years in a hotel room! Who would have believed it?

No less than the Hotel Nacional, which you will see listed in your travel guide as one of the cheapest in Mexico City.

Most likely you will have been lured by the limping manager (El General, Eduardo calls him with a salute), who hawks rooms in the tireless voice of a carnival caller, This way, this way. The bath water is always hot, the rooms are quiet comfortable cheap, the site historic. Here, page 15 of your Baedekers, this is us, El Nacional, built during the reign of Maximillian.

Most likely you will be doubtful, barely able to see through the evening haze thick with diesel fumes, to where the brushstrokes of grays and smears of browns, the soot-streaked stone and grimy windows materialized into El Nacional, now squeezed between buildings equally worn.

Don't be fooled, El General will have said, this was once *un gran edificio*, the Versailles of hotels, its foundation stones taken from a ruined Aztec temple or two by Los Montez, a family on intimate terms with Emperor Maximillian, the ill-fated Viennese gentlemen who danced to music fluted by Napoleon III.

Yes, Eduardo will say when you mention the aging manager's extravagant claims, I know you carried all that luggage to the room by yourself—El General's leg was years ago crushed when a beam fell on it during an earthquake—but formerly there was a full retinue of servants (all Indians, all scandalously underpaid). And such was the power, the prestige of the Church in those once-upon-a-time days that clergymen stayed the night for free.

You will try, but you will not be able to reconcile the velvet-lined memories of El Nacional—stately oil paintings of Mexican *personajes* such as Vicente Guerrero,

Benito Juarez, General Santa Anna (of Alamo fame) stolen to the last; hand-carved chairs with legs bowed as if unable to support the weight of overstuffed emerald-green cushions; candelabra chandeliers—you will not be able to place them next to the buffet in need of refinishing in Eduardo's slightly tilted room.

You will not be able, even in the pliable realm of imagination, to restore the balding carpets in the hallway, the dulled paint in need of dusting and a fresh coat, the water-stained ceilings, the bare-bulb lighting, the brownish tapwater (the Victorian clock with wrought-iron hands has stopped in the lobby but rust marches on in the pipes). Time is a measureless matter of daylight filtering through the exhaust-fume sky, through shades brittle as old newspaper.

IT's a wonder the rain is not black, Eduardo will say. The city is built upon an old lake bed. It would not hold still even when Madero rode in triumphant to end the dictatorship of Porfirio Diaz; streets shook, buildings cracked, roofs tumbled.

On his lopsided buffet, a miracle of warping and water stains that had once floated several city blocks in a flood—on that buffet indescribable via Euclidean geometry, admirable to anyone with van Gogh's eye for disproportions, you will notice, neatly stacked, five or six boxes of Earl Grey Tea.

I would give up Mexico's current form of government, the Republic, Eduardo will say, and live under a restored monarchy to obtain a year's supply.

Then he will smile disarmingly, his teeth yellowed from proximity to too much smoldering tobacco.

A monarchy is rather dashing after all. Not the silliness Iturbide attempted, appointing himself king—where is the divine providence in that?—or Santa Anna and his ill-mannered clownish followers. No, something with dignity.

No doubt you ran into Eduardo in the hotel lobby which, no matter how musty or poorly lighted, is as securely linked by telephone wire to Cairo, Bangladesh, Jerusalem, Passaic, N.J. as to Mexico itself. You were amused by the pompous air of the manager whom you overheard exclaiming that he will breathe his last breath in the service of his guests.

Viva los turistas!

There, while trying to place a long-distance call—your Spanish is not very good—Eduardo probably took the opportunity to introduce himself and offer his services as translator.

Technology, he likes to say, has a way of dangling the improbable before you only to confound you with an insurmountable detail—language for example.

Anomalous Eduardo Lerma, as old as Mexico City permits men to be, will speak English with an Oxford accent, carry a long umbrella and don his bowler as would any gentleman who has grown accustomed to London's fog. At Oxford University, he will not have failed to inform you, he was another in the long legacy of nobility, possessing a scholar's instinct for well-worded truth, a rogue's predilection for women fragrant with the perfume of willingness.

Of all the things he learned there, the one he would take with him if forced to choose—Let us say the planet were coming to an end in a week—is etiquette. No matter when apocalypse strikes, one must be properly dressed for the occasion and be sure to utter words that will be remembered.

Resting his creaky back against a chair in the lobby, Eduardo will direct a comment at the aging manager who steps from past to present, past to present and loses a frame of motion in between—

Digame General, como esta la pierna hoy? Que tiempo pronostica para la semana que viene?

—before inviting you to his room to sip tequila with him. It is not the best brand, he surely will have apologized, leading the way up a staircase so dim, so humid with years, so badly lit, you will imagine for an instant you are in the catacomb stillness of the temple of Quetzalcoatl in Chichen Itza, ascending the breathing wet stone steps that take you to the tiny red idol of a jaguar god, lit in that ancient moss-lined darkness by a single bare bulb.

In any event, tequila is just to make do.

Eduardo would rather a few bottles of a thick Jamaican rum, an island warmth left in the pit of his stomach. Yes, rather than repossess all the land taken during the war of the Alamo, I would rather several bottles of this very wonderful rum. Eduardo will empty his glass with the forlorn grace of a butterfly swept out to sea by mischievous winds.

Oxford, he will say, was a grand experience.

He will pour himself another.

But it was nothing compared to traveling half the length of a country, from Texas to Mexico City, on horseback.

I was a true caballero.

He will talk of the 20,000 pounds sterling—quite something in those days—he had with him with which to finish his education. And the first lady who caught his eye on return to Mexico (ah, she had the cheekbones of an Aztec princess) who was gracious enough to allow him to reduce that sum by a thousand.

There were other women in other cities—Gaudalajara, Chicago, Vera Cruz, New York, Los Angeles—who were just as eager to eat in the finest restaurants and mingle with the sons and daughters of bankers, industrial tycoons, politicians.

Never the same woman for more than a week or two, no matter how beautiful. They all had to have their turn, don't you see?

He will recall nights spent dancing in domed clubs, twice running into Tommy Dorsey's band and once managing, with a flourish, to get an autograph from Glenn Miller for Louise who bore a striking resemblance to Patty, the prettiest of the Andrews Sisters. The music in full swing, he and Louise danced, two art deco silhouettes pressed against the vault of heaven, the stars wheeling overhead, outdone only by the sequin sparkle of her dress. The world was wondrous through a glass of red wine.

What does it matter that 20,000 pounds, enough to last a wise man a lifetime, had bought only six months?

Ah, yes, there was *mi padre*.

A hard man locked in another era, enamored of the flint knives of Aztec priests and the hearts bared to them as offerings to the Sun.

Sacrifice, Eduardo, there is nothing that more ennobles the human spirit.

Although Padre was descended of a wealthy Spanish family, olive-skinned, his thin mustache perfectly trimmed always, a suit and tie even at the breakfast table, he was the kind of man who could live in a hut with an earthen floor if circumstances demanded, eat corn tortillas for breakfast and again for supper, work in the fields from sunup till sundown, the whole time sprinkling the earth with the salt of his sweat.

Discipline, Padre often said, is what separates man from beast, and I respect no man who lacks it. A man must conquer his urges, Eduardo. No one is fat against his will.

No, no Father, I beg to differ. A sip of Earl Grey tea at one's leisure is what separates man from our four-footed friends. Wasn't it Shakespeare, he will turn to you and ask, who said even a beggar is in the poorest thing superfluous?

Disinherited, Eduardo did not take well to routine.

What is a man if he cannot take a nap in the sun when the mood so strikes him?

He will admit that even as a child he was too old to change.

There was never a time when I would permit myself to be anything other than what I was. Though now I must admit that I have become like the descendant of an Aztec ruler: when we dig subways nowadays, we come across the remains of my empire, I cannot help being reminded. So many years have gone by that now they come to only so many old stones. And I must live on top of them.

Certain regrets are acquired tastes, sipped at now and again despite their bitterness.

Sometimes (he will rub his brow with thumb and middle finger) my head hurts all the way to God.

You will see him then as he sees himself, leaning over the faucet in the morning for what one day shall prove to be the last time. Like El General, the manager, he too has lost most of his hair, is not oblivious to the strange smell that is his own, a sourness that no amount of soaping or perfuming can rid him of, the smell of age, the smell he remembers from his grandmother's sweaters when she crushed his child's face to her great stomach; it belongs to him now, is something he can never take off, and no matter how many times he sees the sag in cheeks he keeps meticulously shaven, he will be surprised at how unfaithful his memory has been to his reflection.

If he were not so thin—yes, he will think, his chest is birdlike, is mostly ribs so how did that paunch, a round bloated *pinata*, get there?—he would have jowls.

You will see him wandering the halls early in those mornings, steeped in the settled darkness, through the ill-fitting walls of the hotel, exposing a body that is pear-shaped, sagging over the elastic waist of his baggy boxer shorts, a clownish sight he would be embarrassed to know you can so easily imagine.

You will see him hesitate outside one of the rooms, hearing as he always does the gunshot he never heard in the first place. He will enter that room, searching the peeling wallpaper of faded flowers until he finds the place—to this day you can see the poor job of spackling they did—where one of the bullets disappeared.

I was a child then, the horse more popular than the car. The Nacional was still quite a place, its owner a meek, spiritually minded vegetarian who got ill at the sight of uncooked meat. A wealthy man with a yellowish complexion, he was very popular with the servants, having doubled their wages, infuriating his wife, Olga Luz who, as it turned out, wanted nothing to do with sallow-faced Frederico and sent her lover to kill the poor man in his sleep. Frederico awoke, several shots were fired, and he was killed anyway. Olga Luz and the lover disappeared for all time.

Leaving their children to war among themselves for ownership. The youngest child, Magdalena the Silken Voiced (and that is not all that was rumored to be silken), the daughter of the Olga Luz, was half sister to Wilfredo and Santiago, brothers born of a different mother. She carried on scandalously with Wilfredo, only to leave him for an unhappy American oil man who spent most of his days drinking tequila and most of his nights staring out at the darkness as if Mexico City were at the bottom of the long-vanished lake, as if he were a body adrift in a tide of unhappy memories. The relationship lasted long enough for her to embezzle to her heart's content and divorce him, cleverly having gotten him to keep the hotel in her name.

By then the Nacional had begun to fall into disrepair. Spending the money not on upkeep but on her own frivolities—perfumes at a servant's yearly salary per ounce, dresses adorned with the luster scraped from Africa's deepest mines, men she fancied as she aged whom she attracted with her status and wealth—she found herself alienated from her family, dying at last within her satin sheets, sheltered beneath her canopied bed whose lace coverings made from endless looping hours of work by patient Indian women and their tireless fingers. Magdalena left behind a genuine will proven false—

A bit of legal magic, Eduardo will say bitterly, that would have made a young man who was no Montez owner of El Nacional.

It was not long after Magdalena ascended like the evil saint she was that the first presidential suite was cut up as part of a scheme to create more revenue with more rooms rented out more often. This process continued over the years as the neighborhood grew more crowded, until one morning you woke up to see clothes hanging in that imprecise zone between two buildings and within a week's time several families had squeezed themselves in, diapers were hanging on cords tied to snapped-off broom handles stuck into the ground, to iron fencing, to a sapling struggling in a patch of unpaved earth.

On the city's perimeter, entire villages spring up overnight—*abracadabra*—the new inhabitants praying to the Indian Virgin of Guadalupe to keep the police from evicting them from the harsh land they have claimed, from their uneven rows of lopsided shacks. No straight edges, Mexico is a country without reliable geometry. Stakes and ropes hold things in place, tarpaper keeps the rain out; the lucky ones have cloudy plastic windows flapping in the breeze, blankets or no windows at all for the rest. No sewers, electricity, running water, heat. They pray that the diseases of overpopulation do not take their children who play in the dust of the dirt roads and mark their faces with their own filthy hands, who would not be admitted to the city hospitals without a few pesos to get some orderly's attention. Others live in the city dump, in caves dug into the slopes of piled trash, eyes peering out at you like night creatures caught in the glare of headlights.

Oh these Mexicans are brilliant at improvising, Eduardo will say with a sparkling mixture of condemnation and envy. Look out the window, down on the street, there is the ten-year-old fire-eater Little Lopez, who is discolored from the time he was careless with the fluid, who nearly died when he inhaled. He has gathered a collection of thrown pesos over the years; he is better off than Carlos the streetwalker, the wino, who picks through garbage, warming himself in winters at one of the bonfires made of truck tires, burning in the last of the vacant lots—a lucky thing there is so much rising smoke, the gods can't see what has become of their people.

But I, I am a perfect Christian, Eduardo will tell you. It is an accident I am here. The Spanish would never have come here if not for empty coffers. They cared nothing for calendars with a different measure of time, nor for a mountainous terrain inhabited by a fierce dark people whose religion revolved around the sun.

What can be expected of me, living in a country founded on a rumor passed from conquistador to conquistador, whispering of an Indian emperor who had not been crowned but coated in a fine layer of gold, who plunged into a lake to wash the glittering excess of royalty from him, sent it to grace the murky bottom, who presided over a city that blinded from a distance so that you must never look straight at it, but always out of the corner of your eye? Whose streets turned up gold on the bottoms of sandals?

Can you blame me for wanting a home in Barcelona—I do miss the sea from time to time—a servant or two, and a small but impressive collection of Picassos?

Instead of Picassos, there were wives—much more trouble though no less beautiful—five of them in all.

My first, Isabella, always thought my father would eventually soften and reinstate me as heir. She had the name of a queen and the shrewdness of a sewer rat. As the years went by, Padre showed no signs of weakening, and she left me for another man.

It was all just as well. At the time I was having an affair with Concepcion, my second wife-to-be. Her voice could shatter glass as easily as her looks ruined hearts. I would go to any length to avoid an argument with her. I remember her so well there is no photograph that could be more faithful, a woman of Spanish Aristocracy with henna-colored hair, and her eyes, ah her eyes, were the kind could induce men to point revolvers at one another. It is a shame our love was the crystalline variety—beautiful to the eye, but rather impractical, nothing you could dig a ditch with. One day she gave such a yell it went to a thousand pieces. I was still on my way to another part of Mexico when the echoes died away.

Immaculada accepted me for what I was: a man of simple means with rather extravagant tastes. I met her as she threw seeds to the pigeons outside the Catedral Nacional, its stone the color of bad weather, too monumental to be anything but alienating, God's will done on Earth, the masses cannot be fed why not the pigeons? Why should everything go hungry? A doorway to her heart opened during this act, I stepped in, took off my hat, and there I stayed for a good many years. There I still am sometimes. I cannot say exactly why I left her, but she is the reason I put myself up at the Nacional.

He will laugh so strangely you will be sure at that moment that he has broken with the familiar reality in which forks, knives, trolley buses, television sets are commonplace, and we all agree on their uses.

What fantastic irony, he will say, and the steadiness of his voice will lift you out of the fear of that pit into which you thought you had descended, what fantastic irony that I put myself up here and not one of the thousand other tawdry hotels in this city.

Because you will not understand, he will remind you of Magdalena of the Silken Voice, the Byronic woman who had carried on with a half brother, whose extravagant tastes and frivolous values began the downfall of the Nacional.

She was among those whom I had enchanted while squandering my Oxford tuition. She was, of course, much older than I, but even so, the ruins of empires—Rome, Greece, Egypt, Tenochtitlan—have their own sort of beauty. We were perfectly matched, both well bred, knowing we would never end up married, I using her for her social position, she using me for my youth. She took an extraordinary liking to me. She actually—as far as was possible for her—fell in love with me, I flatter myself to think, this queen of an already eroding glorious past.

He will shake his head and smile sadly because you still do not understand.

I am the young man she willed this place to, only to have her half brothers, Wilfredo and Santiago—nearly dead of old age—arrive on the scene with an army of lawyers and disprove the validity of a perfectly valid will. So I was no better off than Mexico, with the broken promise of wealth brought by oil, of fool's gold.

Here he will dig in the top drawer of the warped buffet and produce a handful of carefully ribboned letters and lavender envelopes, an age of his life meticulously bound, and hold them up as proof.

All in her hand, all signed. It may be these would have swayed the jury in my favor, or perhaps these too would have been discredited, but I withheld them … out of naive faith in justice, out of useless reverence for the unscrupulous dead, out of what is left of *mi padre's* sense of honor—I can't say.

Returning the letters to their wooden vault lined with silence, he will take out another handful of papers, wave them around with his back to you while searching out more papers.

These are how I make my living . . .

He will produce articles typed in English, which one of the city's newspaper pays him a pittance to translate into Spanish.

Without my Oxford English I would be standing next to Carlos smelling of burned rubber during the long winters.

You will realize then what a rare occurrence you are, that the visitors in Eduardo's tiny room are stirrings out of the past, barely brushing aside the curtains as they come and go. You will feel, inexplicably, a degree of the awful stiffness morning brings to Eduardo, the futility of afternoons checking the empty mailbox, the evening remembrances (eyes closed and tequila fumes beginning to efface perception) of friends whose funerals Eduardo has attended—Alberto Gutierrez who struggled through Oxford with Eduardo and went on to become a respected politician, a portrait of him in his small round glasses now hanging in an administrative building in Guadalajara; Pablo Ribalta, El Torito, the Baby Bull, who had *cojones* the size of grapefruits and rode with Pancho Villa when he was 12, no bottle of tequila could withstand his onslaught, what a demon he looked in the meager light of a bar or a brothel—his favorite places to be—with his great long mustaches wet with liquor and sweat pouring down his face, his huge white grin in his dark face, strong as a pack mule but his heart finally burst, all that strength but he too is gone; and most of all Vicente Gonzales, a handsomer kinder more open-hearted man never breathed, nor does he any longer his casket having been laid open by candlelight the old way in the house not in some parlor, his best suit, his bow tie perfectly tied and *Madre de Dios* even dead he looked better than the tear-glistening faces bending over him. Like Eduardo, you will vainly salute young lovers arm in arm on the sidewalk below who cannot see you, you will invite hotel guests (who always seem to have an excuse ready) to share the bottle. And then you will light a cigarette in Eduardo's honor in spite of the surgeon general's warning, instead of a candle.

Yes, this country, once thought to bleed gold when wounded, has proven a dream of dust, far from a source of water now, sitting upon an old lake bed, cut off from the rest of the world by stern-faced mountains. The Sun is hazy on the hottest of days because the fumes create their own weather, their own sky.

And yet they still come, you should see their faces, the *campesinos*, the farmers wearing sandals cut from old tires, bewildered as they step from the bus, used to the emerald green of mountains and the fertile fields they've left, the lowlands and jungles, entirely lost. Benito Juarez should never have shown them what was possible. Now every Oaxacan, every Indian who comes to Mexico City wants to become president, transformed by the crush of city life into a diamond shining through history's darkest moments.

With innocent reverence they gaze up at the handiwork of our artists who have managed to record Mexico's moments of glory, to turn tragedy into wall murals, events into colors—banana yellow, gunshot-wound red, overgrown green, peasant-earth brown, peon white—they turn blood into paint, their oils dry with the faint smell of rusting iron, and the plastered stone wall that had meant nothing a moment ago—other than you will have to go around it—becomes the wailing wall of a country in agony.

The world will never end—look how much it has endured already without even coming close—an apocalypse is just wishful thinking. The only mouth we know is the mouth twisted in pain, the mouth gasping for justice . . . ah, pain is all we know, the loaded rifle all we respect. The painted figures of Rivera and Orozco shout like vainglorious Santa Anna who lost his leg to a French cannonball and never let the Mexican people forget his unwilling sacrifice, exclaiming as he asked to be crowned that his last drop of blood would be bled in the service of his country.

So now you have seen the New World the Europeans set out for. But which is new? The one of the Mayans or the Aztecs? The Zapotecs or the Olmecs? The Toltecs or the Tarahumara? All older by millennia—not years but another kind of time, more nebulous, harder to measure—than Europe. This is the land of the guttural tongue, the great dead stone cities, the legend that has begun to lift itself out of the ruins like those surreal paintings in which the images raise themselves off the canvas, emerging from flat two-dimensional art into the four- or five- or twenty-two-dimensional actuality we cannot keep track of anymore even if we read the latest scientific magazines.

But in truth, these are things for someone of greater stature to worry about, the next Benito Juarez who may be getting off the bus coming from Oaxaca today. If I confine myself to my own worries, my own complaints, Eduardo will say, well, they can be counted on one hand.

Aside from a shortage of import items, he will mention a knee which has never been the same since a fall from a particularly unruly horse. He will cite the Nacional's infamously infrequent hot water (one day I threw open a window and hollered *El Grito del Eduardo* for a steaming shower). At predictable times of the year, he has strange dreams he is certain are somehow linked to what is going on in the mountains, to what does not belong to the city.

A loud uncle with grandiose manners once told me of an Aztec practice—particularly savage in its imagery—in which once every 52 years a fire is turned loose in the chest cavity of a sacrificial victim and all the pots are smashed, all the used vessels, a resurrection. I wonder what kind of coincidence it is that the Pemex building, the seat of the government oil monopoly, is 52 stories high, a monument to air pollution.

A miscellaneous warning, like a stray gunshot, he will point out the window and say, Out there you must be careful of coyotes, the kind without fur.

But it will not be these coyotes he sees in the sunless hours before dawn. It will be the Aztec ritual haunting his poor eyesight. He will be drawn by what is burning, by the hot orange light, the face of a sacrificed human gazing indifferently at the equally indifferent heavens, the two glassy eyes with the red gleam of flame in the pits of their pupils.

Eduardo will straighten his back against the bedboard, he will choose his words with the careful desire to be remembered, those things he would say as the clock strikes, sounding the demise of the world that will not end.

There is a great fire burning in Mexico, he will say, beginning with the tiny ones dowsing the streets in woodsmoke, the cooking fires tended by women in colorful serapes who carry styrofoam begging cups, Carlos and black-smoke-billowing truck tires, the oil out of the earth's plundered insides, the fire roaring inside a hollowed-out human chest—a fire whose source is at the center of our existence, and the smoke that will choke us off in the end.

What we need in Mexico is 20,000 years of solitude at least, and no cars or cutting down jungle for farmland. No foreigners in the rich plant-infested heat, no boats larger than reed-bundle canoes on lazy winding rivers in the Yucatan.

For my own part, I would be able to bear the unheard-of inflation of the peso if only I could afford a fine Jamaican rum to go with my Earl Grey tea. What does it matter, eh? We dedicate ourselves to immortality—there is a little Ozymandias in all of us—but we cannot stick around to bask in it, so who is crazy? If you want to build a monument, pile up the things you have done, a grand and determined accumulation of the women you have loved, the dawns you have greeted with reverence in your heart, the times you swam the Caribbean and had the salt washed from you by a violent thunderstorm. Yes, if life were made of colors mine would arc across the sky after a good thunderstorm.

Still, he will say, breathing a sigh laden with cheap tequila, one goes on wishing.

By the time his chin has dropped toward his chest, he will have lost himself in a vanishing city where on every street corner, graced by a stately wrought-iron gas lamp, is a woman in a sequined dress, the slitted pupils and jade green eyes of a jaguar, a beauty he had once danced with, now a ghost of memory made of shifting light standing silently beside the post with its hissing lamp. You will sense that Eduardo has gone off quietly, his stare into the past a portal to the place where his lover Magdalena awaits, but he will break the spell by turning to you suddenly.

Ah amigo, Eduardo's eyes will hold the dull glow of the sinister fire burning in Mexico, *cada edad tiene su encanto.* Every age, he will repeat with a finger raised, has its enchantment.

JAMES RICHARDSON

Vectors 5.1: Otherwise

The secret to unhappiness is knowing exactly what you want.

•

They make a point of seeming dissatisfied, as if it were less important to love their lives than to prove they aren't fooled by them.

•

Somewhere in the multiverse, the theory goes, some duplicate of me has everything I could imagine wanting. Should that make me happier or sadder?

•

Though it's not what I ordered, I don't say anything. Maybe it won't be great, but it won't be disappointing in quite the way what I chose could have been.

•

I like having choices a lot better than using them.

•

So often it would have been better to doubt my confidence, but I would have needed more confidence in my doubt.

•

Dreams hurt each other.

•

I'm going to start calling it *predicting the Past*, since so much of what I want to know about the Future is how I'll feel then about what I'm deciding to do Now.

•

What's called creativity is an accident we learn to keep having.

•

Luck whispers *You deserved me.*

•

Silly to worry about the freedom of the will since most of me arrives from beyond its reach: weather, history, accident, you.

•

Self-expression? The things that sound exactly like me are exactly what I try to keep myself from saying. You have to run the water a while before it's cool and true.

•

I'm blissfully solitary for a minute—and then who shows up but myself?

•

Let's be fair about the limits of language: often enough what it says is actually better than what we were thinking, though maybe not as good as what we thought we were thinking.

•

It's about as easy to find a truth no one has ever said as a mistake no one has ever made.

•

I tripped so badly I danced.

•

How embarrassing to be a god, stripped of all your excuses. Everyone would know that everything you were, everything that happened to you, everything that came out of your mouth was exactly what you had wished.

•

The unbeliever's prayer: *Help me so subtly I don't notice. Be the luck I can take credit for.*

•

Mountains are always moving. It's less a matter of faith than of patience.

•

Maybe I'm not lost, just a little too certain I should be somewhere else.

•

The road not taken also would have gotten me home.

•

It always makes sense to say *You're alive, what else do you want?* But only to yourself.

VIRGINIA KONCHAN

Pater Noster

Father, Holy Father, Prime Mover, God Almighty—
I have forgotten what to call you.
I have forgotten my pretense,
my sounding board, my ruin.
My friends, are they happy?
My enemies, are they fed?
O apophasis, O singsong lament:
your head will have its halo.
I use my finger to write your name.
Today, I have done nothing
but historicize my feelings:
nothing but inoculate myself
from rabies and airborne ills.
What is not everywhere.
I am smitten with the sun.
Sweet Jesus, Good Shepherd:
the minute the doctor says cancer,
I can think of nothing else.
Cure me of ancestral longing.
Cure me of the need for speed.
I shunt my body into your whereabouts,
Lord, pray for the end of virginity.
I have grown wholesome and wise
in the interstice between centuries,
yet my soul remains morose and blue.
I fasted, love, while others were feasting.
I stood forever holding my hand out to you.

KHALED MATTAWA

Procreation

(Moria Refugee Camp, Lesbos)

Dreams copulate
with our memories. We begin
to have many days of birth,

many mothers. Our fathers'
names branch out like weeds,
God shatters countless like stars.

Don't close your eyes,
or the stories you've told
will swallow you.

Look to your body:
Your skin will be your anchor.
Your scars will never betray you.

NANCY CHEN LONG

6-Phallic (Rorschach Blot)

In seminary, I learned Christianity is in love
with dichotomy—heaven/hell, body/soul,
with us/against us. Life as electrical circuit,

reducible to a unit-step function—1/0, on/off.
Years earlier, studying architecture as art,
when the professor said the church

steeple represented God's penis, I learned that some see
any sharp object with a point as a penis. Men—
sharp, with a point. Women—dull and pointless.

So of course Rorschach inkblot #6 is meant to make
you see genitalia. In it, the penis points up. Below it,

the vulva. The penis, with its single eye,
isn't looking at you. Its gaze is heavenward,

eye on God. It's the vulva that faces you, humanity, wide open
and vulnerable. If everything is didactic, then we learn

by decoding someone else's ink stain. A test
bears the mark of its maker, a blot born of his mind.

The steeple meant to impale the Devil as he falls
is the penis that points the way to God.
Of course it does.

BRENDAN CONSTANTINE

Confirmation

We were told not to look at the angel
in the classroom. At least I think
it was an angel; it was very tall,
had three legs, antlers, and a black
coat. Eyes front, the teacher said,
Stay on your page. All year, the angel
stood at our backs while we wrote,
listening, I was sure, to our blood,
our thoughts, our shy answers
to history. Once, I dared to hint at it;
we'd written our way to Ancient Greece
and I raised my hand for a question.
What, I asked, was the Hellenic word
for messenger? I felt a throb in the air,
as from an open stove. My friends
hushed. The teacher took off his glasses.
And then the bell rang, a full minute
early. There's you're answer, he said.
Next morning, he was gone. The teacher
I mean. We had a new one, a woman
with broad shoulders, a limp. And
the angel's coat was red now,
with buttons shaped like dogs.

CHARLIE CLARK

Devil on What He Does Not Read

Every day I pass the letters of Matthew Arnold,

all six, green volumes, and cannot bring myself to leaf

through what it was to bathe in the chill of an outdoor metal pail

or however it was done in Liverpool, or Dover, in eighteen fifty-

something; it won't do, reading about the small chickens he fed on

with little pleasure; his explanations of verse and god and why

some debt or other need not be paid; other than the day

he watched the porpoises the children threw stones at

go under and never come back, there is so little to read as moral;

the sunrise he said reminded him the world is ending;

how after seeing it and everything touched by its striated beams,

how after admitting he didn't know exactly what *striated* means,

how everything became evidence the world is always ending;

how the heart gives out asking for more soap, a moment, a jar of ripened figs.

Devil Saying Pulchritude

is the ugliest word for *beauty*

is just one way he means to charm you,

the other his lamenting how you like to watch chicken hawks

circle above car lots because it reminds you how things can die anywhere

and not how the clouds they move through only speak of rain,

that really all water ever does is wreck and surrender.

If that doesn't do it, let him tell you

about the lake that got so toxic it turns all that touches it to ash—

let him show you the lynx bent to drink from its thick lip;

even the one stray, imperious flamingo

that winging down to land on it went dead like that,

though in its gray and new-found sheen—

led on by a weak passel of wind—

it did for some time elegantly continue to drift.

ERIKA MEITNER

A Temple of the Spirit

Let's say you are on a plane, and before
the plane rises to clear congregations of
tree-tops and blue-grey mountains,
you watch the woman who called you up
by zone number then scanned your ticket—
you watch her from your plane seat don
a knit cap and head out to the runway to
waive your plane from the gate with two
bright orange batons, her arms held in an
uppercase L as our plane taxis past her
and her fluorescent green safety vest
to rise quickly over the tiny houses and
iced-over cattle ponds of the Eastern Shore.
Let's say that now you are on that plane
thrusting itself deep into clouds which
enshroud everything for a moment in a
dense halo of whiteness that is not fog—
the kind of bright cloudiness you'd expect
from the transition to a movie's dream
sequence or the opening to an episode
of *Highway to Heaven* with Michael Landon
right before he walks down that deserted
canyon road, duffel bag in hand, then hops
in a baby blue 1977 Ford when Victor French
pulls over for him. In the show, Landon is
actually an angel stripped of his wings.
He and French (a retired cop) are given
assignments by The Boss to help troubled
humans overcome their problems. What I'm
saying is sometimes we are asked to arrive
in a new city and assume the identities of
business employees or civil service workers

for the greater good. Or sometimes we are forced
to hold out our arms like cheerleaders for a team
we don't believe in as if our bodies can influence
the score no matter what we are thinking, but
what if the team is humanity? I don't know
if there's a god, but sometimes we are asked
to carry a baton for long periods of time as if
we're in a relay and can hand it off to the
next person waiting usually somewhere other
than the place we began, though that action is
so tricky and fails often. I hope the gate woman
was L for team Lift-off or Levity or Love of the
human race—Luck for our tin can with twin
engines newly cleared of snow. Let's say yes.

Bios

HADARA BAR-NADAV is the author of four poetry collections and two chapbooks, most recently *The New Nudity* (Saturnalia, 2017) and *Fountain and Furnace* (Tupelo, 2016), and co-author of the textbook *Writing Poems, 8th Edition* (Pearson, 2011). The recipient of an NEA Grant in Poetry, she teaches at the University of Missouri—Kansas City.

CHRISTINA BEASLEY's poetry appears in *Hobart, Obsidian, The Pinch*, and elsewhere. She has done residencies with *Atlantic Center for the Arts, Southern Illinois University*, and *Virginia Quarterly Review*, and serves as assistant poetry editor of *Barrelhouse*.

HELENA BELL's fiction has appeared in *Clarkesworld, Lightspeed*, and *Best American Science Fiction and Fantasy*. She lives in Durham, North Carolina.

The recipient of a New York Foundation of the Arts Fellowship in Poetry (2014) and in Fiction (2006), **EMILY BLAIR** is a visual artist who creates multimedia books. Her chapbook is *The Nature of Hairwork* (Dancing Girl, 2019), and her poems have appeared in *The Gettysburg Review, Indiana Review, Brooklyn Poets Anthology*, and others.

DON BOGEN's fifth poetry collection is *Immediate Song* (Milkweed, 2019). The recipient of two Fulbrights and fellowships from the Camargo Foundation and the National Endowment for the Arts, he is an emeritus professor at the University of Cincinnati and serves as editor-at-large for *The Cincinnati Review*.

BRUCE BOND is the author of 22 books, most recently the poetry collections *Frankenstein's Children* (Lost Horse), *Dear Reader* (Free Verse) and *Rise and Fall of the Lesser Sun Gods* (Elixir), all published in 2018, as well as *Blackout Starlight: New and Selected Poems 1997–2015* (LSU, 2017). He teaches at the University of North Texas.

JENNY BROWNE is the author of three poetry collections from University of Tampa Press, most recently *Dear Stranger* (2013). She teaches at Trinity University in San Antonio.

SASHA BURSHTEYN is a writer and photographer who was born in Russia and raised in New York and Ukraine. Her work has appeared in *Calvert Journal, Crannóg Magazine*, and *The Rumpus*.

Recent poems by **CHARLIE CLARK** appear in *New England Review*, *Pleiades*, *West Branch*, and other journals. His collection *The Newest Employee of the Museum of Ruin* is forthcoming from Four Way Books in 2020. He lives in Austin, Texas.

ANDREA COHEN's sixth poetry collection is *Nightshade* (Four Way, 2019). She has received a PEN Discovery Award, *Glimmer Train*'s Short Fiction Award, and several fellowships to the MacDowell Colony. Her work has appeared in *The New Yorker*, *Poetry*, *The Threepenny Review*, and elsewhere. She directs the Writers House at Merrimack College and the Blacksmith House Poetry Series in Cambridge, MA.

Work by **BRENDAN CONSTANTINE** has appeared in *Field*, *Ploughshares*, *Prairie Schooner*, *The Best American Poetry*, and elsewhere. His most recent collections are *Bouncy Bounce* (Blue Horse, 2018) and *Dementia, My Darling* (Red Hen, 2016). The recipient of an NEA Grant, among other awards, he teaches at the Windward School. Since 2017 he has been developing poetry workshops for people with aphasia.

LEIGH ANNE COUCH's first poetry collection is *Houses Fly Away* (Zone 3, 2007), and recent work appears in *The Cincinnati Review*, *Gulf Coast*, *Salmagundi*, and elsewhere. A longtime editor at Duke University Press and the *Sewanee Review*, she now lives in Tennessee.

Recipient of the 2016 Eric Hoffer Best in Small Press Award, **VINCENT CZYZ** is the author of the novel *The Christos Mosaic* (Blank Slate, 2015). His work has appeared in *Boston Review*, *New England Review*, *Shenandoah*, and elsewhere.

MAYA TEVET DAYAN is an Israeli-Canadian poet who received 2018 Israeli Prime Minister Award for Literature and was an "honorable mention" for the 2016 Kugel Poetry Prize. Her poems have been translated into English, Spanish, and German; she holds a PhD in Indian philosophy and literature and translates Sanskrit Poetry. For more information, see page 29.

Originally from Chengdu, China, **SHANGYANG FANG** writes in English and Chinese. The winner of the Gregory O'Donoghue International Poetry Prize and the Joy Harjo Poetry Award, he has published poems in *Narrative*, *Ninth Letter*, *StoryQuarterly*, and elsewhere. He is a poetry fellow at the Michener Center for Writers.

JOHN GALLAHER's sixth poetry collection, *Brand New Spacesuit*, is forthcoming from BOA Editions in 2020. His recent poems appear in *Field*, *New England Review*, *Poetry*, and elsewhere. He lives in rural Missouri and edits *The Laurel Review*.

JENNIFER HABEL is the author of *Good Reason* (NFSPS, 2012), and her work appears in *Alaska Quarterly Review*, *Barrow Street*, *The Common*, and elsewhere. Her second book, *The Book of Jane*, won the 2019 Iowa Poetry Prize and is forthcoming. She coordinates the creative writing program at the University of Cincinnati.

EDWARD HIRSCH's many poetry collections include the forthcoming *Stranger by Night* (Knopf, 2020) and *Gabriel: A Poem* (2014), a book-length elegy for his son. The recipient of a MacArthur Fellowship, among other honors, he directs the Guggenheim Foundation.

Dutch writer **LUCAS HIRSCH** is the author of five poetry collections and a novel. He lives in Haarlem. For more information, see page 65.

TROY JOLLIMORE teaches philosophy at California State University, Chico. He is the author of three poetry collections, most recently *Syllabus of Errors* (Princeton UP, 2015), which was listed as a best poetry book of the year by the *New York Times*.

KIRSTEN KASCHOCK is the author of four poetry collections—most recently *Confessional Sci-Fi: A Primer* (Subito, 2017) and *The Dottery* (Pittsburgh, 2014)—as well as a speculative novel, *Sleight* (Coffee House, 2011). She teaches at Drexel University.

DAVID KEPLINGER's fifth poetry collection *Another City* (Milkweed, 2018) won the 2019 UNT Rilke Prize, and he has co-translated books by Carsten René Nielsen and Jan Wagner, including Nielsen's *Forty-One Objects* (Bitter Oleander, 2019) and Wagner's *The Art of Topiary* (Milkweed, 2017). He teaches in the MFA Program at American University.

PATRICK KINDIG's chapbooks are *all the catholic gods* (Seven Kitchens, 2019) and *Dry Spell* (Porkbelly, 2016), and his poems have appeared in *The Journal*, *Shenandoah*, *Washington Square Review*, and elsewhere. He is a PhD candidate at Indiana University.

Poems by **STEVEN KLEINMAN** appear in *American Poetry Review*, *The Iowa Review*, *Oversound*, and elsewhere. He teaches at the University of the Arts in Philadelphia.

VIRGINIA KONCHAN is the author of the poetry collections *Any God Will Do* (Carnegie Mellon UP, 2020) and *The End of Spectacle* (2018), and the short story collection *Anatomical Gift* (Noctuary, 2017). Her work has appeared in *The New Republic*, *The New Yorker*, *Best New Poets*, and elsewhere. She teaches at Concordia University in Montreal.

MAUREEN LANGLOSS has published fiction in *Gulf Coast*, *The Journal*, *Sonora Review*, *Best Small Fictions*, and elsewhere. She lives in New York and serves as flash fiction editor at *Split Lip Magazine*.

NANCY CHEN LONG has received an NEA Fellowship in Poetry and the Robert H. Winner Award from the Poetry Society of America. Her first book *Light into Bodies* (U of Tampa, 2016) won the Tampa Review Prize; her second book, *Wider Than the Sky* is forthcoming from Diode Editions. She works in the Research Technologies Division at Indiana University.

ALESSANDRA LYNCH is the author of three poetry collections, most recently *Day-lily Called It a Dangerous Moment* (Alice James, 2017). The recipient of the Barbara Deming Award and fellowships from Yaddo, the MacDowell Colony, and the Vermont Studio Center, she teaches at Butler University.

BILL MARSH is a college teacher in Chicago who also tends bees in the Fox River Valley. His work has appeared in *Ascent*, *Bluestem*, *Writing on the Edge*, and elsewhere. From 2005–15 he edited the Heretical Texts book series via Factory School.

A MacArthur Fellow, **KHALED MATTAWA** is the author of four full-length poetry collections and, most recently, the chapbook *Mare Nostrum* (Sarabande, 2019). He has translated numerous poets from Arabic, including Adonis, Mahmoud Darwish, Amjad Nasser, and Saadi Youssef. He teaches at the University of Michigan.

The recipient of an associates of arts degree from Ohio University, **LYLE MAY** is a death row inmate in Raleigh, North Carolina, though Minneapolis is home. His work has appeared in *J Journal*, *Scalawag Magazine*, and on *TheMarshallProject.org*.

JANE MEDVED is the author of *Deep Calls To Deep* (New Rivers, 2017) and the chapbook *Olam, Shana, Nefesh* (Finishing Line, 2014) Recent work has appeared in *The Cortland Review*, *Gulf Coast Online*, *The Tampa Review*, and elsewhere. She is the poetry editor of the *Ilanot Review* and a visiting instructor at Bar Ilan University, in the Shaindy Rudolph Creative Writing Program.

ADAM MEISNER lives in Ottawa, Ontario, where he writes poetry, plays, and fiction. His poems have appeared widely, and in 2018 his play *For Both Resting and Breeding* premiered at Talk Is Free Theatre in Barrie, Ontario.

ERIKA MEITNER's fifth poetry collection, *Holy Moly Carry Me* (BOA, 2018), won the National Jewish Book Award and was shortlisted for the National Book Critics Circle Award. The recipient of a Fulbright to the Seamus Heaney Centre at Queen's University Belfast, she teaches at Virginia Tech.

RUMA MODAK is a well-known poet, playwright, and fiction writer from Bangladesh. For more information, see page 97.

KELLY MORSE's chapbook is *Heavy Light* (Two of Cups, 2016), and her work appears in *The Cincinnati Review, Gulf Coast, Mid-American Review*, and elsewhere. Her translations of Vietnamese poet Lý Đợi have appeared in *Asymptote* and received the Gabo Prize for Translation.

ALICIA MOUNTAIN is the author of the poetry collection *High Ground Coward* (Iowa, 2018), which won the Iowa Poetry Prize, and the chapbook *Thin Fire* (BOATT, 2018). A lesbian poet based in New York, she is the Clemens Doctoral Fellow at the University of Denver.

SHABNAM NADIYA is a Bangladeshi writer and translator based in California. She has published two recent novel translations: Moinul Ahsan Saber's *The Mercenary* (Seagull/U of Chicago, 2018) and Shaheen Akhtar's *Beloved Rongomala* (Bengal Lights, 2018; Seagull/U of Chicago forthcoming).

Work by **JIM RICHARDS** appears in *Poetry Northwest, Prairie Schooner, Southern Poetry Review*, and elsewhere. The recipient of a fellowship from the Idaho Arts Commission, he lives in eastern Idaho's Snake River valley.

JAMES RICHARDSON's poetry collections include, most recently, *During* (Copper Canyon, 2016); *By the Numbers* (2010), which was a finalist for the National Book Award; and *For Now*, which is forthcoming in 2020. He teaches at Princeton.

MIRA ROSENTHAL's poetry collection is *The Local World* (Kent State, 2011), and she has translated two collections by Tomasz Różycki, most recently *Colonies* (Zephyr, 2013), which was shortlisted for the Griffin Prize. The recipient of fellowships from the NEA and Stanford's Stegner Program, she teaches at Cal Poly.

Polish poet **TOMASZ RÓŻYCKI** is the author of ten volumes of poetry and prose, for which he has won numerous literary awards in Poland and abroad. He teaches at Opole University. For more information, see page 135.

Work by **SHAKTHI SHRIMA** appears in *The Adroit Journal, BOAAT, Tinderbox, Best New Poets*, and elsewhere. She lives in Austin.

LUCAS SOUTHWORTH's book *Everyone Has a Gun* (UMass, 2013) won the AWP Grace Paley Prize, and his stories have appeared in *Agni, Alaska Quarterly Review, Tri-Quarterly*, and elsewhere. He teaches fiction and screenwriting at Loyola University Maryland.

DONNA SPRUIJT-METZ's debut chapbook is *Slippery Surfaces* (Finishing Line, 2019), and her poems have appeared in *American Journal of Poetry, Los Angeles Review, Poetry Northwest*, and elsewhere. A former professional flutist, she is a professor of psychology and preventive medicine at the University of Southern California.

CATHERINE STAPLES is the author of *The Rattling Window* (Ashland, 2013), winner of the McGovern Prize, and *Never a Note Forfeit* (Seven Kitchens, 2010). Her poems have appeared in *The Gettysburg Review, The Kenyon Review, Poetry*, and elsewhere. She teaches in the Honors and English programs at Villanova University.

Work by **KARA KAI WANG** has appeared in *The Adroit Journal, Indiana Review, Tri-Quarterly, Best New Poets*, and elsewhere. The recipient of residencies from the Mac-Dowell Colony and the Vermont Studio Center, she is completing her studies in medicine at the University of California San Francisco.

LESLEY WHEELER's books include the poetry collections *Radioland* (Barrow Street, 2015) and *The State She's In*, which is forthcoming from Tinderbox Editions in 2020. Her first novel, *Unbecoming*, is forthcoming from Aqueduct Press. She teaches at Washington and Lee University and serves as poetry editor of *Shenandoah*.

Required Reading

(issue 30)

(Each issue we ask that our contributors recommend up to three recent titles. What follows is the list generated by the writers in issue 30.)

Aria Aber, *Hard Damage* (Shakthi Shrima)

Marina Abramović, *Walk through Walls* (Brendan Constantine)

Nana Kwame Adjei-Brenyah, *Friday Black* (Helena Bell)

Lauren K. Alleyne, *Honeyfish* (Lesley Wheeler)

Pat Barker, *The Silence of the Girls* (Shabnam Nadiya)

Catherine Barnett, *Human Hours* (Alessandra Lynch)

Rick Barot, *The Galleons* (Donna Spruijt-Metz)

Curtis Bauer, *American Selfie* (Mira Rosenthal)

Frank Baumgartner, et al., *Deadly Justice: A Statistical Portrait of the Death Penalty* (Lyle May)

Billy-Ray Belcourt, *This Wound Is a World* (Hadara Bar-Nadav)

Reginald Dwayne Betts, *Felon* (Charlie Clark, Kirsten Kaschock)

Sara Borjas, *Heart Like a Window, Mouth Like a Cliff* (Donna Spruijt-Metz)

Anne Boyer, *A Handbook of Disappointed Fate* (Sasha Burshteyn)

Ana Božičević, *Joy of Missing Out* (Alicia Mountain)

Sarah M. Broom, *The Yellow House* (Kirsten Kaschock)

Jericho Brown, *The Tradition* (Hadara Bar-Nadav)

Anna Burns, *Milkman* (Jenny Browne)

Gabrielle Calvocoressi, *Rocket Fantastic* (Jane Medved)

Julie Carr, *Real Life: An Installation* (John Gallaher)

Elaine Castillo, *America Is Not the Heart* (Kelly Morse)

Anne Anlin Cheng, *Ornamentalism* (Patrick Kindig)

Tiana Clark, *I Can't Talk about the Trees Without the Blood* (Hadara Bar-Nadav)

Andrea Cohen, *Nightshade* (James Richardson)

Teju Cole, *Blind Spot* (Jenny Browne)

Tyrese Coleman, *How to Sit* (Lucas Southworth)

Martha Collins, *Because What Else Could I Do* (Don Bogen)

CAConrad, *While Standing in Line for Death* (Patrick Kindig)

Rob Cook, *Last Window at the Punk Hotel* (Vincent Czyz)

Brittney Cooper, *Eloquent Rage* (Bill Marsh)

Rachel Cusk, *Coventry* (Adam Meisner)

Kyle Dargan, *Anagnorisis* (David Keplinger)

Julia Kolchinsky Dasbach, *The Many Names for Mother* (Erika Meitner)

Lydia Davis, *Essays One* (Troy Jollimore)

Cara Dees, *Exorcism Lessons in the Heartland* (Don Bogen)

Matthew Dickman, *Wonderland* (Steven Kleinman)

Michael Dickman, *Days & Days* (James Richardson)

Timothy Donnelly, *The Problem of the Many* (Virginia Konchan)

Noam Dorr, *Love Drones* (Erika Meitner)

Julie R. Enszer, Ed., *Sister Love: The Letters of Audre Lorde and Pat Parker 1974–1989* (Alicia Mountain)

Silvia Federici, *Witches, Witch-Hunting, and Women* (Sasha Burshteyn)

Camonghne Felix, *Build Yourself a Boat* (Emily Blair)

Richard Gessner, *The Conduit and Other Visionary Tales of Morphing Whimsy* (Vincent Czyz)

Jeff Goodell, *The Water Will Come* (Erika Meitner)

Peter E. Gordon, *Adorno and Existence* (Bruce Bond)

Michael Hofmann, Ed., *W. S. Graham* (Charlie Clark)

Michael McKee Green, *Fugue Figure* (Khaled Mattawa)

Jessie Greengrass, *Sight* (Jennifer Habel)

Robert Hass, *Summer Snow* (Troy Jollimore)

Maria Dahvana Headley, *The Mere Wife* (Shabnam Nadiya)

Anthony Ray Hinton, *The Sun Does Shine* (Lyle May)

Kim Hyesoon, *Autobiography of Death*, trans. Don Mee Choi (Don Bogen)

Daisy Johnson, *Everything Under* (Shabnam Nadiya)

Patrick Johnson, *Gatekeeper* (Khaled Mattawa)

Ilya Kaminsky, *Deaf Republic* (Maureen Langloss, Nancy Chen Long)

Doris Kareva, *Days of Grace*, trans. Miriam McIlfatrick-Ksenofontov (Shangyang Fang)

David Keplinger, *Another City* (Bruce Bond)

Elizabeth Kolbert, *The Sixth Extinction: An Unnatural History* (Brendan Constantine)

Laila Lalami, *The Other Americans* (Mira Rosenthal)

Lance Larsen, *What the Body Knows* (Jim Richards)

Shayla Lawson, *I Think I'm Ready to See Frank Ocean* (Patrick Kindig)

Kiese Laymon, *Heavy* (Leigh Anne Couch, Bill Marsh)

Jill Lepore, *These Truths: A History of the United States* (Edward Hirsch)

Paige Lewis, *Space Struck* (Brendan Constantine)

Yiyun Li, *Where Reasons End* (Edward Hirsch)

Ada Limón, *The Carrying* (Jim Richards, Shakthi Shrima)

Matthew Lopez, *The Inheritance* (Adam Meisner)

James Lough & Alex Stein, Eds., *Short Circuits: Aphorisms, Fragments, and Literary Anomalies* (Jim Richards)

Rose McLarney & Laura-Gray Street, Eds., *A Field Guide to Southern Appalachia* (Lesley Wheeler)

Sabrina Orah Mark, *Wild Milk* (Kirsten Kaschock)

Jane Mead, *To the Wren: Collected and New Poems* (Andrea Cohen, Alessandra Lynch)

Erika Meitner, *Holy Moly Carry Me* (Jane Medved)

Yukio Mishima, *Patriotism*, trans. Geoffrey W. Sargent (Shangyang Fang)

Jose Luis Moctezuma, *Place-Discipline* (Bill Marsh)

Rosalie Moffett, *Nervous System* (Jennifer Habel)

Jenny Molberg, *Refusal* (David Keplinger)

Catherine Gilbert Murdock, *The Book of Boy* (Leigh Anne Couch)

Michael Nardone, *The Ritualities* (Virginia Konchan)

Maggie Nelson, *Something Bright, Then Holes* (Leigh Anne Couch)

Diana Khoi Nguyen, *Ghost of* (Steven Kleinman, Kelly Morse)

David Orr, *Dangerous Household Items* (James Richardson)

Michelle Penaloza, *Former Possessions of the Spanish Empire* (Kara Kai Wang)

Hai-Dang Phan, *Reenactments* (Lesley Wheeler)

Carl Phillips, *Wild Is the Wind* (Donna Spruijt-Metz)

Sarah Pinsker, *Sooner or Later Everything Falls into the Sea* (Helena Bell)

John Poch, *Texases* (Catherine Staples)

Kevin Prufer, *How He Loved Them* (Alessandra Lynch)

Lia Purpura, *All the Fierce Tethers* (Shakthi Shrima)

Paisley Rekdal, *Nightingale* (Catherine Staples)

Karen Russell, *Orange World and Othe Stories* (Christina Beasley)

Diane Seuss, *Still Life with Two Dead Peacocks and a Girl* (Nancy Chen Long, Jane Medved)

Natalie Shapero, *Hard Child* (Steven Kleinman)

Brenda Shaughnessy, *The Octopus Museum* (Christina Beasley)

Kent Shaw, *Too Numerous* (John Gallaher)

Sandra Simonds, *Atopia* (Virginia Konchan)

Emily Skaja, *Brute* (Nancy Chen Long)

Monica Sok, *A Nail that Evening Hangs On* (David Keplinger)

Joshua Sperling, *A Writer of Our Time: The Life and Work of John Berger* (Vincent Czyz)

Gerald Stern, *Galaxy Love* (Alessandra Lynch)

Souvankham Thammavongsa, *Cluster* (Adam Meisner)

Hannah Sullivan, *Three Poems* (Jennifer Habel)

Arthur Sze, *Sight Lines* (Kara Kai Wang)

Nhã Thuyên, *un\\martyred: [self-]vanishing presences in Vietnamese poetry* (Kelly Morse)

Allison Titus, *Sob Story: The History of Crying* (Christina Beasley)

Miriam Toews, *Women Talking* (Maureen Langloss)

Olga Tokarczuk, *Drive Your Plow over the Bones of the Dead*, trans. Antonia Lloyd-Jones (Charlie Clark)

Cadwell Turnbull, *The Lesson* (Helena Bell)

Esmé Weijun Wang, *The Collected Schizophrenias* (Mira Rosenthal, Kara Kai Wang)

Jackie Wang, *Carceral Capitalism* (Sasha Burshteyn)

D. Watkins, *We Speak for Ourselves: A Word from Forgotten Black America* (Lucas Southworth)

David Welch, *Everyone Who Is Dead* (Lucas Southworth)

Tara Westover, *Educated* (Lyle May)

Sarah Wetzel, *The Davids Inside David* (Jane Medved)

Allison Benis White, *Please Bury Me in This* (Bruce Bond)

Eleanor Wilner, *Before Our Eyes: New and Selected Poems, 1975–2017* (Catherine Staples)

Keith S. Wilson, *Fieldnotes on Ordinary Love* (Donna Spruijt-Metz)

C. D. Wright, *Casting Deep Shade: An Amble* (Jenny Browne)

Xi Chuan, *Notes on the Mosquito: Selected Poems*, trans. Lucas Klein (Shangyang Fang)

Jenny Xie, *Eye Level* (Khaled Mattawa)

Yanyi, *The Year of Blue Water* (Emily Blair)

Dean Young, *Solar Perplexus* (Troy Jollimore)

Adam Zagajewski, *Slight Exaggeration*, trans. Clare Cavanaugh (Edward Hirsch)

Kate Zambreno, *Screen Tests: Stories and Other Writing* (Emily Blair)

Diego Zúñiga, *Camanchaca*, trans. Megan McDowell (Maureen Langloss)

The Copper Nickel Editors' Prizes

(est. 2015)

(Two $500 prizes are awarded to the "most exciting work" published
in each issue, as determined by a vote of the *Copper Nickel* staff)

Past Winners

fall 2019 (issue 29)

Derek Robbins, poetry
Sam Simas, prose

spring 2019 (issue 28)

Catherine Pierce, poetry
Sarah Anne Strickley, prose

fall 2018 (issue 27)

Jenny Boychuk, poetry
Farah Ali, prose

spring 2018 (issue 26)

Cindy Tran, poetry
Gianni Skaragas, prose

fall 2017 (issue 25)

Sarah Carson, poetry
Meagan Ciesla, prose

spring 2017 (issue 24)

Ashley Keyser, poetry
Robert Long Foreman, prose

fall 2016 (issue 23)

Tim Carter, poetry
Evelyn Somers, prose

spring 2016 (issue 22)

Bernard Farai Matambo, poetry
Sequoia Nagamatsu, prose

fall 2015 (issue 21)

Jonathan Weinert, poetry
Tyler Mills, prose

spring 2015 (issue 20)

Michelle Oakes, poetry
Donovan Ortega, prose

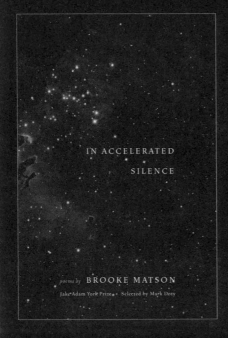

subscription rates

For regular folks:

one year (two issues)—$20
two years (four issues)—$35
five years (ten issues)—$60

For student folks:

one year (two issues)—$15
two years (four issues) $25
five years (ten issues)—$50

For more information, visit: www.copper-nickel.org

To go directly to subscriptions
visit: coppernickel.submittable.com

To order back issues, email wayne.miller@ucdenver.edu